Gold EXPERIENCE

First for Schools

T0350558

Exam
Practice

Pearson Education Limited
Edinburgh Gate
Harlow
Essex CM20 2JE
and Associated Companies throughout the world.

www.pearsonelt.com/exams

First published 2016
ISBN: 978-1-292-14836-6

Set in Arial
Printed and bound by L.E.G.O. S.p.A. Italy

Photo acknowledgements
The publisher would like to thank the following for their kind permission to reproduce their photographs:

(Key: b-bottom; c-centre; l-left; r-right; t-top)

Fotolia.com: EpicStockMedia 50t, Monkey Business 52b, pershing 52t;
Pearson Education Ltd: Gareth Boden 53b, Tudor Photography 49t, 53t;
Shutterstock.com: Andresr 50b, Stephen Girimont 17, My Life Graphic 36, Nejron Photo 34, Pierre-Yves Babelon 8, Audrey Snider-Bell 12, Stocksnapper 14, Vixit 39; **Sozaijiten:** 49b

All other images © Pearson Education

Contents

Exam Overview

The **Cambridge English: First for Schools** exam, also known as the **First Certificate in English for Schools (FCE for Schools)**, is made up of four papers, each testing a different area of ability in English. The Reading and Use of English paper carries 40% of the marks, while Writing, Listening, and Speaking each carry 20% of the marks. There are five grades. A, B and C are pass grades; D and E are fail grades. If a candidate's performance is below Level B2, but is within Level B1, the candidate will receive a Cambridge English certificate stating that they demonstrated ability at Level B1.

Reading and Use of English	1 hour 15 minutes
Writing	1 hour 20 minutes
Listening	40 minutes (approximately)
Speaking	14 minutes (for each pair of students)

All the examination questions are task-based. Rubrics (instructions) are important and should be read carefully. They set the context and give important information about the tasks. There is a separate answer sheet for recording answers for the Reading and Use of English and Listening papers.

Paper	Format	Task focus
Reading and Use of English 7 tasks, 52 questions	**Part 1:** multiple-choice cloze. Choosing which word from a choice of four fits in each of eight gaps in the text.	Choice of vocabulary and relationships between words.
	Part 2: open cloze. Writing the missing word in each of eight gaps in the text.	Grammar, vocabulary and knowledge of expressions.
	Part 3: word formation. Choosing the form of the word given so that it fits into the gap in the text, with a total of eight gaps.	Grammatical accuracy and knowledge of vocabulary and expressions.
	Part 4: key word transformations. Using a key word to complete a new sentence which means the same as the one given, with a total of six pairs of sentences.	Grammatical accuracy and knowledge of vocabulary and sentence structure.
	Part 5: multiple-choice questions. Answering six four-option multiple-choice questions based on a text.	Reading for detailed understanding of the text.
	Part 6: gapped text. Choosing sentences to fit into the gaps in a text, with a total of six sentences to place correctly.	Reading to understand text structure.
	Part 7: multiple matching. Deciding which of the short extracts or paragraphs contains given information or ideas and matching these with ten prompts.	Reading to locate specific information, detail, opinion and attitude.

Paper	Format	Task focus
Writing 2 tasks	**Part 1:** compulsory task. Using given information to write an essay of 140 to 190 words.	Writing for an English teacher, using a formal style.
	Part 2: choice of options. Producing one piece of writing of 140 to190 words from a choice of the following: a letter/email, a story, a review or an article. There is also a question on a set text, which can be an article, a letter, a review or an essay.	Writing for a specific target reader, using appropriate layout and register.
Listening 4 tasks, 30 questions	**Part 1**: multiple-choice questions. Eight short recordings each with a three-option multiple-choice question.	Understanding gist, detail, function, purpose, attitude, etc.
	Part 2: sentence completion. One long recording with ten sentence-completion questions.	Locating and recording specific information.
	Part 3: multiple matching. Set of five short recordings on the same theme to match to one of eight prompts.	Understanding gist and main points.
	Part 4: multiple-choice questions. One long recording with seven three-option multiple-choice questions.	Understanding attitude, opinion, gist, main ideas and specific information.
Speaking 4 tasks	**Part 1:** examiner-led conversation.	Giving personal information, using social language.
	Part 2: individual long turn with visual and written prompts.	Organising discourse in a 'long turn', describing, comparing, giving opinions.
	Part 3: two-way conversation between candidates with written prompts.	Sustaining an interaction, expressing, justifying and exchanging ideas, agreeing and disagreeing.
	Part 4: discussion on topics related to Part 3.	Expressing and justifying ideas, agreeing and disagreeing.

Practice Test 1 with Guidance

Parts 1–4

About the paper

The *Reading and Use of English* paper lasts for 1 hour and 15 minutes. There are seven parts, and a total of fifty-two questions. The reading texts vary in length, and there is a range of text types and styles of writing, for example, extracts from newspapers, magazines, websites and novels. The paper tests your ability to read and understand different types of text, as well as your knowledge of vocabulary and grammar.

Part 1: Multiple-choice cloze

You read a short text. Eight words or phrases have been removed from the text. For each gap, you have to choose from four options the word or phrase that fits best in each gap.

Part 2: Open cloze

You read a short text. Eight words have been removed from the text. You have to complete the gaps using a single word.

Part 3: Word formation

You read a short text. Eight words have been removed from the text. You are given the base form of each missing word at the end of the line, and you have to put that word into the correct form to fit the gap.

Part 4: Key word transformations

You read six pairs of sentences. Both sentences in each pair have the same meaning, but the meaning is expressed in different ways. Two to five words have been removed from the second sentence, and one of these words, the key word, is given to you to use in the answer. You have to complete the second sentence, using the key word, so that it means the same as the first sentence.

How to do the paper

Part 1

- Read the title and the text, ignoring the gaps, to get a general understanding of what it's about.
- Some questions focus on linking words which test your understanding of the whole text.
- Go through the text carefully. Read the options (A–D) for each question. Only one option fits the gap.
- Check the words before and after each gap. This is important because some words can only be followed by one particular preposition.
- If you're not sure which word to choose, decide which options are clearly wrong, and then see which are left. If you're still not sure, you can guess. You don't lose extra marks for wrong answers, and your guess may be right.
- When you have finished, read the whole text again and check that your answers make sense.

Part 2

- Read the title and the text, ignoring the gaps, to get a general understanding of what it's about.
- Think about the missing words. You only need one word for each gap, usually a grammatical word, for example, a pronoun, linker, preposition, etc., or a collocation or phrasal verb.
- Read the text immediately before and after each gap and think about what type of word is missing, for example, a preposition, pronoun, part of a fixed expression, etc.
- Remember to check the whole sentence as well, in case the missing word is a connector.
- When you have finished, read your completed text again and check that it makes sense.

Part 3

- Read the title and the text, ignoring the gaps, to get a general understanding of what it's about.
- Decide what type of word is needed in each gap, for example, a noun, adjective, adverb, and whether it is singular or plural, positive or negative. Remember to read the whole sentence containing the gap, not just the line.
- Look at the word in capitals to the right of the gap. You may need to add a prefix or suffix, or make other changes. You may also need to make more than one change.
- When you have finished, read your completed text again and check that it makes sense.

Part 4

- Read the sentence carefully and think about what it actually means.
- Look at the key word. What type of word is it? What usually follows it, for example, an infinitive, a preposition, or could it be part of a phrasal verb?
- Think about any other words that might need to be changed in the new sentence, for example, an adjective may become a noun.
- Your answer may include words or expressions that were not used in the first sentence, but these must express exactly the same idea. Don't include any new information, or change the information or meaning of the sentence.
- Use between two and five words, and remember that contracted words count as two words, for example, *won't* = *will not*.

Parts 5–7

About the paper

Part 5: Multiple choice

There is one long text to read. You have to answer six questions, each with four options. The questions follow the order of the text.

Part 6: Gapped text

You read one long text from which six sentences have been removed. These are placed in jumbled order after the text, along with an extra sentence that does not fit into any of the gaps. You have to use your knowledge of grammar, vocabulary, referencing and text structure to put the six sentences into the correct place in the text.

Part 7: Multiple matching

There is either one long text that has been divided into sections, or a series of short texts all on the same topic. There are also ten prompts which report information and ideas from the text(s). You have to match each prompt to the correct text or section of text.

How to do the paper

Part 5

- Read the title and text quickly to get a general understanding of what it's about and how it's organised.
- Read through the questions or question stems without looking at the options (A–D), and underline key words.
- The questions follow the order of the text. Find the piece of text where a question is answered and read it carefully, underlining key words and phrases.
- Some questions which test vocabulary or reference skills will tell you the line where the targeted word or phrase can be found. Read the sentences before and after the one including this word or phrase to find the answer.
- Try to answer the question yourself. Then read the four options (A–D) and choose the one that is closest to your own idea. Look for the same meaning expressed in different ways in the text and in the options.
- Check that the other options are all clearly wrong. If you are still unsure, read the text again very carefully and look for reasons why some options may be wrong.

Part 6

- Read the title and text first, ignoring the gaps and the options, to get a general understanding of what it's about and how it's organised.
- Carefully read the text around each gap and think about what type of information might be missing.

- Read sentences A–G. Check for topic and language links with the text. Highlight reference words and words that relate to people, places, events and any time references. This will help you follow the development of the argument or narrative.
- Choose the best option to fit each gap. Make sure that all the pronouns and vocabulary references are clear.
- Once you've finished, read through the completed text to be sure that it makes sense with the answers in the gaps.

Part 7

- You don't need to read the whole text or texts first. The text contains some information that you don't need to answer the questions.
- Read the prompts (43–52) first, underlining key words and ideas. Think about the exact meaning of each one.
- Read through the text(s) quickly and find information or ideas that relate to each prompt.
- When you find the relevant piece of text for each prompt, read it very carefully to make sure it completely matches the meaning of the prompt.
- The ideas in each prompt are likely to occur in more than one section of the text, but only one text exactly matches the idea or meaning of the prompt.

Part 1

For questions **1–8**, read the text and decide which answer (**A**, **B**, **C** or **D**) best fits each gap. There is an example at the beginning (**0**).

In the exam, you mark your answers **on a separate answer sheet**.

Tip strip

Question 2: This is a preposition that goes with 'compare'.

Question 4: Think of a phrasal verb that means 'to leave on a journey'.

Question 5: You need a word that means 'a short journey'.

Question 8: You need to think of a complete phrase that means 'it's difficult to believe'.

Example:

| 0 | **A** in | **B** for | **C** into | **D** at |

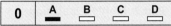

Castaway?

Have you seen the movie *The Life of Pi*? It is a fictional tale about a young man shipwrecked **(0)** .... a storm and stranded in the middle of the ocean on a lifeboat. He faces thirst and starvation until he learns how to **(1)** .... fish to eat and collect rainwater to drink. But Pi's adventures are nothing compared **(2)** .... real-life castaway José Ivan who, it appears, **(3)** .... at sea for thirteen months before being found alive and relatively well on a small Pacific island.

José claims he **(4)** .... out from Mexico, 12,500 kilometres away, with one companion. They were intending to go on a one-day shark-fishing **(5)** .... , but their small boat was hit by a **(6)** .... As the boat's engines didn't **(7)** .... any more, the two men had to go where the sea took them. Sadly José's companion died after four months at sea. But José lived on a diet of seabirds, fish and turtle blood. While some fishermen **(8)** .... it hard to believe that a little boat could have floated so far across the ocean, experts say it is just possible. As for José, all he wants is to be reunited with his family.

1	**A** take	**B** tempt	**C** catch	**D** attract
2	**A** at	**B** to	**C** by	**D** for
3	**A** survived	**B** overcame	**C** lasted	**D** continued
4	**A** put	**B** went	**C** left	**D** set
5	**A** voyage	**B** trip	**C** travel	**D** journey
6	**A** wind	**B** breeze	**C** storm	**D** flood
7	**A** act	**B** work	**C** drive	**D** operate
8	**A** find	**B** think	**C** claim	**D** suggest

Tip strip

Question 9: This word introduces a relative clause, and refers to 'a robot'.

Question 11: Read the sentence after the gap, which contrasts with the previous one.

Question 12: Think of a way of giving an example of something.

Question 14: You need a preposition that goes with 'affected'.

For questions **9–16**, read the text below and think of the word which best fits each gap. Use only **one** word in each gap. There is an example at the beginning (**0**).

In the exam, you write your answers **IN CAPITAL LETTERS on a separate answer sheet**.

Example: | 0 | H | A | V | E | | | | | | | | | | | | | | | | | | | | | |

The most advanced robot ever

Scientists in the USA **(0)** .... just designed a robot called Atlas **(9)** .... may turn out to be one of the most advanced humanoid robots ever built.

Seven teams of scientists are working on building **(10)** .... physical shell of the robot and then plan to give it a software 'brain'. **(11)** .... its inventors claim its purpose is to help in rescue missions, some people fear the robot could be used as a **(12)** .... of artificial soldier. Whatever the truth of this, one advantage is that the robot would be able to venture into regions **(13)** .... humans could not survive, such as those areas affected **(14)** .... nuclear radiation. Another plus is that Atlas is very strong, and can keep its balance even **(15)** .... being hit by a 9-kilogram demolition machine or extreme storms.

However, its designers assure us that the robot is intended for domestic situations. One of these could be to help elderly people in **(16)** .... own homes. So, what may be the most advanced robot ever is set to improve people's lives.

Tip strip

Question 18: Can they see the dog now, or not? What prefix do you need to use?

Question 19: Did she think that she will ever find her pet?

Question 20: You need the noun form of the word.

Question 24: Think about a fixed phrase that means *it's obvious*.

Part 3

For questions **17–24**, read the text below. Use the word given in capitals at the end of some of the lines to form a word that fits in the gap **in the same line**. There is an example at the beginning (**0**).

In the exam, you write your answers **IN CAPITAL LETTERS on a separate answer sheet**.

Example: | 0 | M | I | S | S | I | N | G | | | | | | | | | | | | | | | | |

The missing dog

A dog which had been **(0)** .... for nine long years has finally	**MISS**
been **(17)** .... with its owner, Jessica Brown. The animal had	**UNITE**
escaped from Jessica's garden and immediately **(18)**	**APPEAR**
Jessica was heartbroken, but as time passed she knew it was	
increasingly **(19)** .... that she would ever see her pet again.	**LIKE**
So, when she got a phone call to say the dog had been found	
eighty kilometres away, she greeted the news with absolute	
(20) .... A policeman had seen the dog wandering around	**ASTONISH**
the streets and **(21)** .... for Jessica, had checked its microchip.	**FORTUNATE**
This showed who it belonged to and **(22)** .... the policeman to	**ABLE**
contact Jessica. The dog was in **(23)** .... good condition after	**SURPRISE**
such a long time, in spite of its ordeal. **(24)** .... to say, both dog	**NEED**
and owner were delighted to see each other once again.	

Tip strip

Question 25: Ben's teacher said 'don't forget' so it 'reminded him' to do it.

Question 26: You need three words to complete the expression meaning 'in an isolated area'.

Question 28: Think about the grammar that follows 'allow' and 'let'.

Question 30: 'instead' + preposition has the same meaning as 'rather than', but what form follows it?

For questions **25–30**, complete the second sentence so that it has a similar meaning to the first sentence, using the word given. **Do not change the word given**. You must use between **two** and **five** words, including the word given. Here is an example (**0**).

Example:

0   My brother had a really good idea for our next holiday.
     CAME
     My brother ……………………………………………… really good idea for our next holiday.

The gap can be filled with the words 'came up with a', so you write:

Example: | **0** | CAME UP WITH A |

In the exam, you write only the missing words **IN CAPITAL LETTERS on a separate answer sheet**.

---

25   'Ben, don't forget to switch off the computer,' said his teacher.
     REMINDED
     Ben's teacher ……………………………………………… the computer.

26   The place we camped was in a very isolated area.
     BEATEN
     The place we camped was ……………………………………………… track.

27   We couldn't climb the mountain because of its great height.
     HIGH
     The mountain was ……………………………………………… climb.

28   They didn't let Clare go to the disco.
     ALLOWED
     Clare ……………………………………………… go to the disco.

29   I started dancing two hours ago.
     HAVE
     I ……………………………………………… hours.

30   Paul put his money in the bank rather than spend it.
     INSTEAD
     Paul put his money in the bank ……………………………………………… it.

You are going to read an article from a magazine about the conservationist Steve Irwin. For questions **31–36**, choose the answer (**A**, **B**, **C** or **D**) which you think fits best according to the text.

In the exam, you mark your answers **on a separate answer sheet**.

Steve Irwin, the crocodile hunter!

One of the people I most admired when I was a teenager was an Australian wildlife expert called Steve Irwin. The easy way he handled the scariest of wild animals was just amazing. He would risk his life quite regularly as he did spectacular feats such as fighting to control alligators. He was also chased by komodo dragons, faced venomous snakes which could kill with one bite, and he crept up silently behind lions. Sitting in front of the TV, you could escape from your boring life to a world of adventure as you watched him perform these awesome activities.

line 8

Some people criticised Steve. They said he was just a showman and that he did stupid things with animals just to make himself famous. What his critics didn't realise, however, was by filming these breathtaking scenes, Steve was able to fight for animal conservation and educate people in a very powerful way. His passion for wild creatures was clear and his sense of excitement and enthusiasm spread to most of those who watched him. Because of his close relationships with the animals he handled, he could predict their behaviour and that is how he could act in such a crazy way with them. For teenagers like me, he made wildlife conservation really cool!

Everything about Steve was the opposite to what you first imagined. People called him 'The Crocodile Hunter' – but instead of ending up as handbags or on a restaurant menu, the crocodiles Steve caught were relocated to somewhere they could live safely. He danced and played with dangerous wild animals that would scare you or me to death – but he said that the most frightening experience of his life was his wedding! So which of the creatures he handled made him most nervous? Parrots, he confessed, although how these brightly coloured birds could scare him more than crocodiles is hard to understand!

His passion for animals began early. His parents devoted all their free time to rescuing local wildlife and returning it to the wild. Steve was given a snake for his sixth birthday and was soon following in his father's footsteps and learning to capture these venomous reptiles for himself. In later life he probably became one of the most knowledgeable reptile experts in the world. Capturing crocodiles was his next challenge; he became so good that he could stand on a crocodile's back, close its jaws (containing rows of sharp teeth) in his bare hands and then tie the jaw up with rope. He spent many months in deserted areas of Australia catching problem crocodiles before hunters could shoot them. The techniques he developed are now used around the world.

Steve's adventures with animals and his message about wildlife conservation brought the subject to life for me in a way that my biology classes never could. Although some Australians got angry with Steve – they said he made people think all Australians said 'Crikey' and were brave but stupid – I knew they were wrong about him. I also knew he'd bought thousands of acres of land so he could save habitats for endangered wildlife and spread the message about conservation. My big ambition was to travel to Australia and see some of his work in action. But fate prevented this.

It was perhaps not surprising that one day Steve's luck would run out. It happened while he was making a film called *Ocean's Deadliest* and swam over to film a stingray. A stingray is a large flat fish which has a dangerous sting at the end of its tail. The creature does not normally attack humans unless it is under attack. Steve must have alarmed it in some way and sadly a sting from the fish killed the man least likely to harm it. He died at the age of just forty-four doing what he loved most, spreading his message about how wonderful wild creatures were. And because of all he managed to achieve in his short life for this important cause, he is my greatest inspiration.

Tip strip

Question 31: Think about the word 'venomous'. Are these snakes dangerous?

Question 32: Look for what the writer says about Steve, not what other people say about him.

Question 35: Look for why some Australians got angry with the way Steve behaved.

Question 36: Think about why Steve was unlucky.

31 The word 'venomous' in line 8 means

   A harmless.

   B poisonous.

   C tame.

   D painful.

32 In Paragraph 2, the writer says that Steve

   A acted stupidly with animals.

   B was only interested in fame.

   C disagreed with some conservationists.

   D wanted to educate people.

33 It appears from Paragraph 3 that Steve

   A never caught crocodiles himself.

   B wasn't truthful about himself.

   C didn't share most people's fears.

   D refused to keep some kinds of birds.

34 The writer uses the example of the crocodile's jaws to show

   A how strong Steve had become.

   B how good Steve's skills were.

   C how dangerous Steve's job was.

   D how many risks Steve took.

35 According to the writer, some Australians

   A weren't impressed by Steve's courage.

   B believed that Steve was brave but stupid.

   C didn't share Steve's passion for wildlife.

   D didn't like the way Steve portrayed himself.

36 In Paragraph 6, we learn that the creature that attacked Steve

   A was killed by his companion.

   B is not usually aggressive.

   C often hunts alone.

   D didn't mean to harm him.

You are going to read a magazine article about the plays of William Shakespeare. Six sentences have been removed from the article. Choose from the sentences **A–G** the one which fits each gap (**37–42**). There is one extra sentence you do not need to use.

In the exam, you mark your answers **on a separate answer sheet**.

The magic of Shakespeare

If you ask anyone to name their top twenty famous names from history, they will probably include William Shakespeare in their list. In fact, Shakespeare has become one of the most important cultural icons, or representatives, that the British possess. People sometimes suggest that Shakespeare's plays deal so closely with the time and place in which he wrote (England, in the 1600s) that they can have little meaning for people who live in other parts of the world. **37 ▢**

Take the world of politics, for example. Shakespeare often rewrote historical events and folk tales in order to explore particular themes, including state corruption, i.e. government officials acting dishonestly for money; he also explored the use of state violence. At the time he was writing, it was extremely dangerous to criticise anyone in authority. Anyone who did so could end up imprisoned in the Tower of London! **38 ▢** It was therefore very important for him to find clever ways of dealing with political issues without annoying the authorities and getting into trouble. People find this fascinating, particularly if they come from countries where it is dangerous to speak about certain topics in public.

39 ▢ This became clear recently, when theatre companies from around the world gathered in London to perform their own presentations of his plays. The productions were amazing. Although they'd been translated into other languages, Shakespeare's words kept all their magic. And everybody identified with the plots, which deal with themes of love, hatred, jealousy and revenge as well as politics. I knew one of the foreign theatre companies quite well. I had flown to their country some months before to direct a play they were rehearsing at that time. The actors were students and came from a very poor district where crime and violence were common. The play they were due to perform was *Measure for Measure*.

40 ▢ To my surprise, their production was funnier, but more disturbing, than any versions of the play I've seen in England. What made these actors understand the themes of the play so well, I wondered? I soon discovered the reason.

41 ▢ That's why they understand what the play is saying more than many British theatre-goers. It also helps them see why Shakespeare wrote the plays as he did, with scenes that suddenly jump from comic to tragic. These actors saw that Shakespeare was portraying what actually does happen in real life; sometimes you can stand up and fight corruption in a serious way – but if this puts you in too much danger, you have to make fun of it and attack it in that way. British people know about violence and corruption too, of course. Young British people whose friends or family have been killed out of jealousy or for revenge can understand and identify with the plots of plays like *Romeo and Juliet*.

42 ▢ They used all the experience they'd ever gained to make his stories live for their audience and to make them laugh one minute and cry the next. They were just superb!

A Every day these young actors live through real-life experiences that are actually quite similar to the ones Shakespeare is portraying.

B But what surprised me about this group of overseas actors, was how willing they were to forget the fact that, for them, Shakespeare was a 'foreign' writer and how keen they were to use their lives to explore his ideas.

C As a playwright, Shakespeare risked being punished as much as everyone else in the country.

D There are other ways in which Shakespeare's plays have meaning for people outside his native country.

E However, experience shows that the playwright's work has just as much meaning for foreigners as it has for citizens of his native country.

F I wondered how well they would understand this play, which is one of the darkest of Shakespeare's comedies.

G However, Shakespeare's plays do not always have meaning for people in a different time or place.

Tip strip

Question 37: Look for a sentence that contradicts the suggestion that Shakespeare's plays have little meaning for some people.

Question 39: Look for an example of other ways in which Shakespeare's plays have meaning for people outside his native country – the text mentions companies from around the world.

Question 40: Look for the name of the play that is referred to when the writer says 'this play'.

Question 41: Look for a sentence that provides a reason for why the actors 'understand what the play is saying'.

Tip strip

Question 43: Look for a paragraph that talks about how to survive on Mars.

Question 45: Look for a paragraph that mentions the high cost of space travel.

Question 46: Look for a paragraph that talks about science-fiction predictions that were not fulfilled.

Question 51: Look for a paragraph comparing manned and unmanned space travel.

You are going to read an article about space travel. For questions **43–52**, choose from the paragraphs (**A–D**). The paragraphs may be chosen more than once.

In the exam, you mark your answers **on a separate answer sheet**.

Which paragraph mentions

robots being programmed to make more copies of themselves?	43
the idea of carrying out a long-term project?	44
being prevented from travelling by financial difficulties?	45
being disappointed that fiction wasn't fact?	46
the possibility of making a permanent home on Mars?	47
altering the gasses surrounding a planet?	48
providing suitable accommodation on Mars?	49
finding proof that there is ice or snow on a planet?	50
a reduction in space expeditions involving humans?	51
increasing the physical enjoyment of space travel?	52

Destination Mars!

A

When scientists announced they had landed a robot space vehicle on Mars for the very first time, back in the 1970s, the news was amazing. Although this spacecraft or 'probe' had no humans on board, it was equipped with cameras and other equipment which enabled it to take measurements and send information back to Earth. One of the most exciting things the probe did was search for signs of life on the planet. Science-fiction writers have often written about alien creatures living on Mars and many of us rather hoped they existed. Sadly none were found, although scientists did discover evidence of frozen water. Since that first exploration, similar unmanned probes have travelled huge distances, to the Sun, Moon, and nearly every other planet in our galaxy, sending back exciting information that has greatly increased our knowledge of the solar system and its inhabitants.

B

However, while unmanned space missions to the planets have increased in number, the same is not true for human space travel. The last human mission to the Moon – and the last time any human walked on its surface – was back in 1972. After that, interest in such voyages seemed to die. This may have been because countries couldn't afford the huge sums of money involved, or maybe because they thought there was little else for humans to discover on the Moon. The chances of humans exploring faraway planets like Mars seemed small. Humans need food, water and air to survive in space as well as shelter from extreme temperatures. The economic and technical problems involved in transporting them to other planets are therefore enormous. Keeping them alive after they land is even more of a challenge.

C

Yet, experts predict that, in the future, engineers may not just be sending humans to Mars; they may even be able to transform the planet into a place where humans can stay! It will take a long time to do this – maybe even hundreds of years. There are many difficulties, of course. Mars is much further from Earth than the Moon and takes far longer to reach. A manned Mars spacecraft would need to be more comfortable than the ones that humans have used so far. It would have to be larger, too, to carry all the food, water and supplies humans would need during the voyage.

D

There is hardly any oxygen for humans to breathe on Mars and the solar winds would soon kill any human who was unprotected from them. In order to survive for long on Mars, humans would therefore need a special building or shelter to live in. Inside the building, they could grow plants, which would provide oxygen for them to breathe and also food for them to eat. But who could actually survive for long enough on Mars to construct such a building? The answer to that question may surprise you – intelligent robots! These robots would be designed in such a way that they could reproduce themselves, using materials from the planet! Once the robots had constructed the dome, plants could be grown and chemicals could be introduced. The result of all this would be to change the type and the amount of gasses on the planet and make it similar to what we have on Earth. And if that happened, humans could emigrate to Mars, just like some people emigrate to Australia now!

Parts 1 and 2

About the paper

The *Writing* paper lasts for 1 hour and 20 minutes. There are two parts to the paper and in each part you have to complete one task.

Part 1

Part 1 is compulsory. You are given an essay title and some ideas. You have to write an essay in a formal style, giving your opinion on the essay title, using all the ideas given and adding an idea of your own. You should write between 140 and 190 words.

Part 2

In Part 2, you must choose one question from a choice of four. Tasks may include the following: an article, an email, a letter, a story or a review. There is also a question on a set text that you can choose to answer if you have studied it, which can be an article, a letter, a review or an essay. You should write between 140 and 190 words.

Task types for Part 2

• Letter or email
• Article
• Story
• Review
• Essay

For more information about the writing paper task types, refer to the Writing Bank on pages 58–64.

How to do the paper

Part 1

• Don't be in a hurry to start writing. Spend a few minutes planning because, then, your answer will be more organised. Read the instructions carefully and make sure you understand:
  – the topic you had discussed in class and the title of the essay you have to write.
  – what information you have to include in your answer: remember you must include both the two notes provided.
• Think of a third point of your own, something which is not mentioned in the two points given.
• Look again at the three written notes, including your own idea, and expand on them by noting down a couple of ideas or details for each.
• Decide how many paragraphs you will need and which ideas you want to group together in each paragraph. Think about how you will connect these ideas.
• When you finish, check through your work. Have you included all the notes? Is it easy to follow? Are there any basic spelling or grammar mistakes that you can correct? Have you written a good conclusion?

Part 2

• In Part 2, you need to choose from task types that may require a semi-formal or informal style, and a variety of formats.

• Look carefully at each task (for example, the review) and topic (for example, a film) and:
  – think of a review. Are you confident you know how to write the task type?
  – think of a film as a topic. Do you have some interesting language you can use?
• Choose a topic where your answers to both of the questions above is 'yes'. For example, choose the review only if you know how to present and organise the information, and you also like the topic and have some interesting language you can use. Make sure you check the question on the set text, as you may be able to answer this.
• Read the task you have chosen and be sure you understand the following:
  – What is the <u>situation</u>?
  – <u>Who</u> will read your piece of writing?
  – What is your <u>purpose</u> in writing this piece?
• Note down the ideas that come into your head, in any order. Then choose your best ideas and decide how you will organise them into paragraphs.
• When you finish, check through your writing. Have you used a range of language? Are your ideas clearly expressed?

Testing focus

Both parts carry equal marks. Spelling and punctuation, length, paragraphing and legible handwriting are taken into account in both parts of the test.

The examiner will consider the following:

content: Have you included all the information required? Is what you have included relevant to the task, i.e. are the points clearly connected with the task?

organisation: Have you organised your writing so that the different paragraphs and sentences are connected logically? Have you used a range of linking words and phrases?

language: Have you used a range of language, including vocabulary, some complex structures and different tenses?

communicative achievement: Have you communicated your ideas in an effective way that holds the reader's attention?

Part 1

You **must** answer this question. Write your answer in **140–190** words in an appropriate style.

In the exam, you write your answer **on a separate answer sheet**.

---

1   In your English class, you have been talking about space travel. Now your English teacher has asked you to write an essay for homework.

Write your essay using **all** the notes and giving reasons for your point of view.

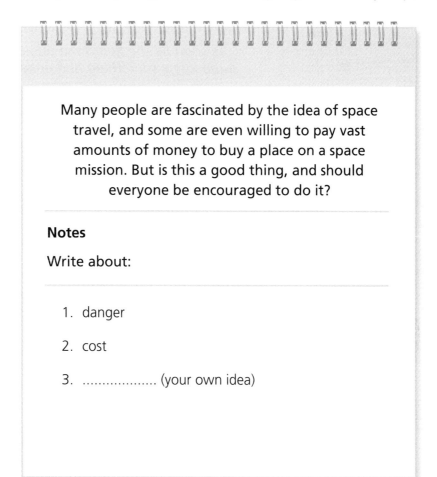

Many people are fascinated by the idea of space travel, and some are even willing to pay vast amounts of money to buy a place on a space mission. But is this a good thing, and should everyone be encouraged to do it?

Notes

Write about:

1. danger

2. cost

3. .... (your own idea)

Tip strip

- Begin by underlining the key words in the instructions, for example, 'Do you think everyone should be encouraged to do this', 'using **all** the notes'.
- Read the essay question and the two written prompts. Note down a couple of ideas to include for each prompt, and also some interesting vocabulary you may use. For example, for the first prompt, you could jot down

'technical problems' and 'distance from help'. Think of a third idea of your own, for example the challenge people like to face, exploring new horizons, extending boundaries, and make some notes on that too.

- Spend a few minutes planning your answer. Remember that the time you spend planning your essay is not wasted time! Decide which ideas you will include in each paragraph.

- Introduce the topic in the first paragraph. You can do this by rephrasing the essay question, for example, 'It's becoming more common for people to go into space, but is this a good idea?'
- Use a variety of tenses and grammatical structures, and some interesting vocabulary.

- The final paragraph is important because it is the conclusion of your argument. Summarise the points you made in previous

paragraphs briefly, then give your opinion clearly.

- When you have finished, check that you have dealt with the two notes provided, and added a point of your own. Check that you have written between 140 and 190 words, but don't waste time counting every word.

- Finally, check your grammar and spelling.

Tip strip

- Read all the questions carefully before choosing one to answer. Simply liking a task type may not be enough. You also need to have some ideas and enough vocabulary for the topic.
- Before you start, remember what you have learnt about that task type. For example, choose Question 2 if you like writing stories and have ideas about how to make them interesting.
- Before you start writing, note down the main points you want to include and plan your answer.

Question 2: Think about what could have happened before or after the phone call and plan your narrative. For example, she could have been planning to meet someone, but they have had a problem. Try to think of interesting vocabulary to use, and have a surprising ending.

Question 3: Use an informal style, but don't use words commonly found in text messages, for example, 'lol'. Your email must have opening and closing lines, and full sentences. Plan your answer: for example, in paragraph 1, say what you and your friends like to do in your free time, and in paragraph 2, explain why you enjoy these activities.

Question 4: Think of the style needed when you write a review. Underline key words in the task, for example, 'what kind of movie', 'what scenes you most enjoyed' and 'why it would appeal to other people of your age'. Jot down some vocabulary you may want to use. Remember, it is a review, so you'll have to give your final opinion at the end.

Question 5: Decide which character to write about, then make notes on examples from the book that you can use to support your opinions. This particular task is an essay, so you need to write a conclusion.

Write an answer to **one** of the questions 2–5 in this part. Write your answer in **140–190** words in an appropriate style.

In the exam, you write your answer **on a separate answer sheet**. Put the question number in the box at the top of the answer sheet.

2   You have seen this announcement in a teen magazine.

> ### Stories wanted
> We are looking for stories for our English-language teen magazine. Your story must **begin** with this sentence:
>
> **As soon as she heard the phone ring,**
> **Anna knew something had gone wrong.**
>
> Your story must include: • a mobile phone
>   • a journey

Write your **story**.

3   You have received an email from your American friend, Paul.

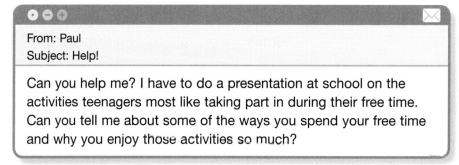

From: Paul
Subject: Help!

Can you help me? I have to do a presentation at school on the activities teenagers most like taking part in during their free time. Can you tell me about some of the ways you spend your free time and why you enjoy those activities so much?

Write your **email**.

4   You see this announcement in an English-speaking magazine for film fans.

> ### Reviews wanted: Favourite Movies
> *Do you have a favourite movie*
> *that you would recommend other teenagers to see?*
> Write a review of the movie, explaining what kind of movie it is,
> what scenes you most enjoyed watching
> and why you think it would appeal to other people of your age.

Write your **review**.

5   Answer the following question based on the title below.

> ### The Eagle of the Ninth by Rosemary Sutcliff
> In your English class, you have been discussing the story of *The Eagle of the Ninth*.
> Now your teacher has given you this essay title for homework:
> Which character do you find most interesting in *The Eagle of the Ninth* and why?

Write your **essay**.

Parts 1–4

About the paper

The *Listening* paper lasts about 40 minutes and has four parts, with a total of thirty questions. There are texts of varying lengths and types, for example, extracts from media broadcasts and announcements, as well as everyday conversations. You will hear each recording twice. You have time to read the questions before you listen.

Part 1: Multiple choice

You listen to eight unconnected extracts of around 30 seconds each. The extracts may be monologues or dialogues, and will include a range of speakers and contexts. You have to answer one multiple-choice question with three options on each extract. Each question tests a slightly different skill, for example, you may be asked to identify a speaker's main point, opinion, feeling or attitude, or whether two speakers agree with each other.

Part 2: Sentence completion

You listen to one long text of around 3 minutes. You will hear one speaker giving a talk or presentation on a specific topic. You read ten sentences which report on some of the main

points from the listening, but a word or short phrase has been removed from each sentence. You have to listen and fill in the missing word(s). The task tests your ability to identify and record specific information.

Part 3: Multiple matching

You hear five short monologues of around 30 seconds. Each speaker is talking on the same topic. There are also eight options to read. As you listen, you decide which option matches each speaker. There are three options you don't need to use. This task tests your ability to understand the gist of what people are saying.

Part 4: Multiple choice

You listen to one long text of around 3 minutes. This is generally an interview or a discussion between two people. You listen and answer seven multiple-choice questions with three options. This task tests your ability to understand detail, including the main speaker's attitudes, feelings and opinions.

How to do the paper

Part 1

- The eight extracts are not linked in any way.
- Before you listen to each extract, look at the context sentence. Think about who the speaker is and what the context is, for example, is it a broadcast interview, an informal chat?
- Read the question and options, and think about what the question is actually asking. Some questions:
  - ask you to identify the speaker's opinions. Before you listen, identify which of the speakers you are listening for and underline key words in the question.
  - focus on whether the speakers agree or not, so you need to listen carefully to both.
  - ask you to identify a speaker's feeling or attitude, or purpose in talking, for example, to explain, to apologise, etc.
  - test your understanding of a speaker's main idea, or a detailed piece of information that they give.
- Listen the first time to find the correct answer to the question yourself.
- Listen again to match that answer to the correct option (A–C).

Part 2

- Before you listen, read the rubric and think about the context.
- You have time to read through all the sentences before you listen. Think about the type of information that is missing.
- Most answers are concrete pieces of information, for example, proper nouns or numbers.
- The information on the page follows the same order as the information in the listening text. Use the sentences to help you keep your place as you listen.
- The words you need to write are heard in the recording. Don't try to change the form of the words or to find a paraphrase – write what you hear.
- Don't write too much in each gap. Most answers will be single words or compound nouns.

- Check that your answer fits grammatically, for example, singular or plural, correct tense, etc., and that it makes sense in the complete sentence.

Part 3

- There are five different speakers all talking about the same topic. You hear all five of them once and they are all repeated a second time.
- You have time to read the task and all the options (A-H) before you listen.
- The first time you listen, pay attention to the speaker's main idea. Mark the option closest to this idea. Remember, the five speakers are all talking about the same topic, so you will hear the same vocabulary and similar information each time, but only one option will match each speaker.
- The second time you listen, check your answers. Remember that there are three options that you don't need to use.
- Don't worry if you don't understand every word you hear. You've probably understood more than you think. If you're not sure of an answer, then guess.

Part 4

- Before you listen, read the instructions and think about the context.
- You have time to read through the questions before you listen.
- Underline key words in the question stems and options.
- The questions follow the order of the recording. Listen for the interviewer's questions that introduce the topic of each question.
- Listen the first time to find the correct answer to the question yourself.
- Listen again to match that answer to the correct option (A–C).
- The words in the options may not be the same as those you hear in the recording. Think about the meaning of what the person is saying and the question you're being asked, then find the best match.

Part 1

You will hear people talking in eight different situations. For questions **1–8**, choose the best answer (**A**, **B** or **C**).

Tip strip

Question 1: The man talks about general rules in the park, though he doesn't use the word 'regulations'.

Question 3: Think about the meaning of 'it's just not on'.

Question 4: Several problems are mentioned, but only one concerns the doctor.

Question 6: Listen for the main purpose of the report and the information it gives.

1 You hear two people talking about a safari park.
What does the man say the park should do?

 A Try to clarify the regulations.
 B Make it easier to see the animals.
 C Pay more attention to safety.

2 You overhear someone leaving a telephone message.
Why is she calling?

 A To ask her friend to contact someone.
 B To cancel an arrangement.
 C To ask a favour.

3 You hear a professional actor talking about her career.
How do her fans sometimes annoy her?

 A By photographing her friends.
 B By making her late for things.
 C By behaving rudely to her.

4 You hear a doctor talking about her work.
What worries her most about the present situation?

 A People don't like telephone appointments.
 B People are becoming more ill.
 C People are not keeping appointments.

5 You overhear a conversation in a school corridor.
What does the boy say about the football practice?

 A It's postponed until next month.
 B It's important for him to attend.
 C It's uncertain because of the weather.

6 You hear a report on the radio.
What is its purpose?

 A To provide a detailed weather forecast.
 B To report on an accident.
 C To give information about travel.

7 You overhear someone leaving a message on his friend's phone.
What is he worried about?

 A Keeping a secret.
 B Paying for something.
 C Misunderstanding information.

8 You hear a writer talking about her work.
What is she doing?

 A Describing her working day.
 B Explaining the success of her novel.
 C Complaining about her publisher.

Tip strip

Question 9: Several numbers and dates are mentioned, but only one is the date the wildlife sanctuary opened for visitors.

Question 12: Listen for something that surprised Christie. You won't hear the word 'surprised', but there is another expression that shows she was surprised.

Question 14: You need to listen for the word Christie uses about the bands, not the other students.

Question 18: You should listen for an expression that shows Christie was disappointed.

Part 2

You will hear a girl called Christie giving a presentation about a school trip to a wildlife sanctuary. For questions **9–18**, complete the sentences with a word or short phrase.

School trip to a wildlife sanctuary

Christie was surprised that it was only since

(9) .... that people could visit the sanctuary.

Christie was sad to hear that in the past people caught birds to get their

(10) ....

Christie was particularly enthusiastic about the

(11) .... at the education centre.

Christie was very surprised by the amount of

(12) .... made by the birds.

Christie was worried when she heard young birds had

(13) .... that could be dangerous.

Christie thought the bands that were attached to the birds resembled

(14) ....

Christie had not expected the changing (15) ....

of a bird to be important to conservationists.

According to Christie, all the students found it difficult to locate where the birds'

(16) .... were.

Christie decided to get round the wildlife sanctuary by

(17) .... because it was kind to the environment.

Christie was disappointed that doing (18) ....

was impossible because of the weather.

Tip strip

Speaker One: Listen for a speaker who talks about how to succeed at being a top ballerina.

Speaker Two: Listen for someone who sent a recording to a ballet school.

Speaker Three: Listen for a speaker who talks about how they started to dance.

Speaker Four: Only one speaker talks about changing their mind.

Speaker Five: One speaker talks about problems they had at ballet school.

You will hear five short extracts in which people are talking about dancing. For questions **19–23**, choose from the list (**A–H**) how each speaker feels about their experience of dancing. Use the letters only once. There are three extra letters which you do not need to use.

A I had to give up dancing for a while.

Speaker 1   [**19**]

B At the start I didn't think ballet was appropriate for me.

Speaker 2   [**20**]

C I got advice from another dancer.

Speaker 3   [**21**]

D I worked hard to be as good as the others.

Speaker 4   [**22**]

E I needed to stand out from the crowd to succeed.

Speaker 5   [**23**]

F Ballet is the most difficult form of dance you can do.

G It was music that first inspired me to dance.

H I made a recording of myself dancing.

Part 4

You will hear an interview with a well-known actor called Paul Little. For questions **24–30**, choose the best answer (**A**, **B** or **C**).

Tip strip

Question 24: Paul mentions all the options, but only one is the reason he became an actor.

Question 27: Listen for something related to his future.

Question 28: Listen for his attitude to reviews and whether they are important to him.

Question 29: He has feelings about all the options, but only one makes him angrier than anything else.

24 Why did Paul choose to become an actor?

    A He felt he was born to do it.

    B His parents encouraged him.

    C He didn't know what other career to follow.

25 Why does Paul believe it's worth going to drama school?

    A You get a lot of practice on the stage.

    B You can learn from your peer group.

    C You get used to dealing with lack of success.

26 Paul feels that auditions are

    A enjoyable because he can show off his talent.

    B important for teaching him the need to be persistent.

    C useful for making contact with other actors.

27 How does Paul feel about playing the same role for a long time?

    A Concerned it might limit the parts he gets in future.

    B Afraid of getting bored with his character.

    C Nervous about having problems with other actors.

28 What does Paul think about reviews?

    A He never reads them.

    B He doesn't approve of them.

    C He doesn't want to judge them.

29 According to Paul, the most annoying thing during a performance is

    A hearing mobile phones ring.

    B being able to see the audience.

    C noticing people arriving late.

30 What does Paul find most difficult about being famous?

    A Having his photograph taken at special events.

    B Being stopped in the street by fans.

    C Losing his privacy in the media.

Parts 1–4

About the paper

The *Speaking* test has four parts and lasts 14 minutes. There are two candidates and two examiners. One examiner acts as interlocutor and interacts with the candidates and the other examiner acts as assessor and does not join in the conversation. The candidates are assessed on grammar and vocabulary, discourse management, pronunciation and interactive communication over the whole test.

Part 1 (2 minutes)

Testing focus: Candidates have to show that they are able to use everyday social and interactional language, such as answering questions about themselves and their interests. It's important to use natural language and not to prepare speeches.

Procedure: The examiner asks candidates questions in turn about their own lives, focusing on areas such as their daily life, leisure, work, future plans, holidays, likes and dislikes. This is a natural way to begin the test and it allows candidates to feel comfortable. The examiner addresses each candidate in turn and the candidates should not talk to each other in this part.

Part 2 (4 minutes)

Testing focus: This part tests the candidates' ability to speak for one minute without any support. They should produce language appropriate to the task, organising their ideas clearly and coherently. They should try to use some complex language forms, different tenses, linking words, etc.

Procedure: Each candidate speaks for about one minute without interruption. The examiner gives each candidate two pictures, and reads a task which is written above the pictures. Candidates always have to compare the pictures, and then say something else about them. When the candidate has finished speaking, the examiner asks the other candidate a question about the same pictures, but they only need to give a brief answer.

Part 3 (4 minutes)

Testing focus: This part tests the candidates' ability to take part in a discussion. They should start the discussion, respond to their partner's comments, and invite their partner's opinions. Candidates will have to work together agreeing, disagreeing, justifying their ideas and giving reasons.

Procedure: The instructions for Part 3 are given in two parts.

First, the examiner reads a question and gives the candidates a sheet with the same question and five written prompts, which they should use to help their discussion. The examiner asks the candidates to talk to each other about the question and the different written prompts for about two minutes. The candidates are given 15 seconds to read the task before starting their discussion.

Then, after two minutes, the examiner reads a second question related to the first task, and gives the candidates one minute to make a decision about this question. When making their decision, candidates should give reasons for their choices. There is no right or wrong answer and candidates won't be penalised if they don't manage to reach a decision. The important thing is the discussion.

Part 4 (4 minutes)

Testing focus: This part tests the candidates' ability to engage in a discussion and to deal with issues in more depth than in earlier parts of the test. Candidates are expected to use a range of grammar and vocabulary when expressing ideas and opinions. It's important to note that they will be assessed on their use of language, not on the opinions they express.

Procedure: The examiner asks the candidates questions related to the points discussed in Part 3, which broaden the topic and allow the candidates to discuss issues in more depth. The examiner may address some questions to both candidates (it does not matter who answers first), or to each of them individually. The candidates should interact with each other in this part, and develop each other's ideas.

How to do the paper

Part 1

Listen carefully to the examiner's questions.

Give interesting answers, with interesting details, reasons, or examples, but don't say too much – your answers should be relevant, but not too long.

Part 2

First, compare the two pictures, pointing out similarities and differences.

Then, move to the question written above the pictures.

Part 3

First, say as much as you can about the issues suggested by the written prompts. Don't be afraid to give opinions and make comments, agreeing or disagreeing with your partner. You don't have to talk about all the prompts – it's more important to have a good discussion about the ones you have ideas about.

Then, when you're asked to make a decision, remember there are no right or wrong choices and that you won't be given marks on your opinions but on the language you produce.

Part 4

Answer questions in depth and express your opinions clearly. If you're not sure what to say you can always ask your partner.

Involve your partner in the discussion – it's good to agree or disagree with what they say.

Good morning/afternoon/evening. My name is … and this is my colleague … .

And your names are?

- Where are you from, *(Candidate A)*?
- And you, *(Candidate B)*?

First, we'd like to know something about you.

Select one or more questions from any of the following categories, as appropriate.

Free time

- **What do you like to do in your free time? (Why?)**
- **Do you prefer to spend your free time on your own or with friends? (Why?)**
- **Are you going to do anything special this weekend? (Why/Why not?)**
- **How much homework do you have to do in the evenings?**

Communication

- **How do you like to find out what's happening in the news? (Why?)**
- **What do you usually do on your mobile phone?**
- **How often do you watch television? (Why?)**
- **How do you like to contact your friends?**

Musical entertainment

- **Do you often go to musical concerts? (Why/Why not?)**
- **Do you read magazines about musicians? (Why/Why not?)**
- **Would you like to play a musical instrument? (Why/Why not?)**
- **Who's your favourite musician? (Why?)**

Tip strip

Free time

Question 3: Your answer may be 'yes' or 'no', but don't forget to give examples of what you could do.

Question 4: Don't spend time thinking about the exact amount of homework you have, just talk! Remember, the examiner is only interested in the language you produce. For example, you could talk about times when you have too much homework.

Communication

Question 1: This may be information about people, events, the environment, etc. For example, you could talk about how you like to get information for schoolwork: whether you listen to the news, read newspapers, find the latest news online or hear news from your parents.

Question 4: You could talk about contacting your friends for different reasons for example, texting for a quick message or using social media to give personal news.

Musical entertainment

Question 2: You could mention different magazines where you read about musicians, or any blogs or tweets you read instead. You could give an example of a musician you like to read about.

Question 3: You could mention an instrument you play already, or say why you would like to learn a different one. It's fine not to want to play an instrument – just give reasons why!

Tip strip

Candidate A: Compare the photographs by saying things like: *Both the sporting activities are outside, but one looks more energetic than the other. The runners are clearly taking it very seriously, but the footballers are just relaxing.* Then answer the question by saying things like: *The runners have chosen to do it with friends so that they can support each other, but the footballers are with their friends to have a good time and have fun.*

Candidate B: Compare the photographs by saying things like: *The people in the top picture are at the seaside, whereas the others are having a holiday in the city.* Then answer the question by saying things like: *The family at the beach are all enjoying the relaxation and the couple in the city seem to be enjoying exploring a new place and seeing exciting things.*

In this part of the test, I'm going to give each of you two photographs. I'd like you to talk about your photographs on your own for about a minute, and also to answer a question about your partner's photographs.

(Candidate A), it's your turn first. Here are your photographs. They show **people doing different sporting activities with friends.** [*Turn to the pictures on page 49.*] I'd like you to compare the photographs, and say **why you think the people have chosen to do these sporting activities with friends.** All right?

(1 minute)

Thank you. *(Candidate B)*, **which of these activities would you prefer to do with friends? (Why?)**

(30 seconds)

Thank you. Now, *(Candidate B)*, here are your photographs. They show **people having a holiday in different places.** [*Turn to the pictures on page 50.*] I'd like you to compare the photographs and say **what you think people are enjoying about having a holiday in these places.** All right?

(1 minute)

Thank you. *(Candidate A)* **which of these holidays would you prefer to go on? (Why?)**

(30 seconds)

Thank you.

Make sure you discuss the advantages and disadvantages of each prompt **before** you move to the next one, for example, *It's a good idea to visit a museum because they have so many exhibits and can give a lot of information, but they can be rather boring and you don't see anything live. It may not be useful for showing the effects of tourism.*

When you have to make a decision, don't repeat what you have already said – try to consider which idea is the **most** useful. You can add other ideas of your own if you like.

Tip strip

Question 1: Think about whether schools do 'enough' to educate students about the environment. You may want to say what happens in your school as an example.

Question 2: Think about the wildlife in your own country, and what tourists can see or do there. You can give examples of what you enjoy, too.

Question 3: Think of times when tourism might be good for the environment, for example, tourists bring money into an area so more can be spent on protecting the environment.

Part 3 (4 minutes)

Now I'd like you to talk about something together for about two minutes.

I'd like you to imagine that a teacher wants her students to find out how tourism affects the environment. Here are some things she is thinking of doing, and a question for you to discuss. First, you have some time to look at the task. [*Turn to the task on page 51.*]

(15 seconds)

Now, talk to each other about **the advantages and disadvantages of doing these things to find out how tourism affects the environment.**

(2 minutes)

Thank you. Now you have about a minute to decide **which would be the most useful thing to do to find out how tourism affects the environment.**

(1 minute)

Part 4 (4 minutes)

Use the following questions in order, as appropriate:

- **Do schools do enough to teach students about the environment? (Why/Why not?)**

- **What do you think a tourist interested in wildlife would enjoy most in your country? (Why?)**

- **Is tourism always bad for the environment, do you think?**

- **Do you think it's a good idea to volunteer to do things to help the environment, like clear up rubbish? (Why/Why not?)**

- **Do you think everyone should be encouraged to recycle everything? (Why/Why not?)**

- **Do young people generally do enough to help the environment in your country? (Why/Why not?)**

Thank you. That is the end of the test.

Select any of the following prompts, as appropriate:

- **What do you think?**
- **Do you agree?**
- **And you?**

Practice Test 2

Part 1

For questions **1–8**, read the text and decide which answer (**A**, **B**, **C** or **D**) best fits each gap. There is an example at the beginning (**0**).

In the exam, you mark your answers **on a separate answer sheet**.

Example:

0 **A** or   **B** either   **C** nor   **D** neither

0	A	B	C	D

Using the Internet

Most teenagers I know are able to access the Internet **(0)** .... at school or at home on a variety of devices such as laptops, phones and tablets.

There are many things they can do on the Internet, including research for homework, but the most popular tends to be accessing a wide variety of **(1)** .... networking sites. This is because they provide a convenient way for teenagers to keep in **(2)** .... with friends throughout the day.

There are clearly many advantageous ways of using the Internet, including entertainment. Teenagers often like to listen to music **(3)** .... travelling by bus or walking to school. It's interesting that CDs are becoming **(4)** .... popular because teenagers prefer to listen to music on their mobile phone or tablet and so **(5)** .... their music from a website.

One drawback of the Internet is the amount of advertising. Most teenagers hate **(6)** .... bombarded with advertisements and choose to disable pop-ups on their device. Even if they do allow adverts, teenagers usually claim they **(7)** .... little attention to them.

So, is using the Internet generally a good thing? **(8)** .... there are many benefits, it may be that it has become so much a part of life that it is difficult for some people to exist without it!

1	**A** friendly	**B** social	**C** companion	**D** common
2	**A** touch	**B** contacts	**C** reach	**D** hand
3	**A** throughout	**B** as	**C** during	**D** while
4	**A** less	**B** rather	**C** very	**D** somewhat
5	**A** download	**B** tag	**C** link	**D** paste
6	**A** going	**B** seeing	**C** being	**D** having
7	**A** pay	**B** do	**C** allow	**D** send
8	**A** However	**B** Although	**C** Given	**D** In spite of

Part 2

For questions **9–16**, read the text below and think of the word which best fits each gap. Use only **one** word in each gap. There is an example at the beginning (**0**).

In the exam, you write your answers **IN CAPITAL LETTERS on a separate answer sheet**.

Example: | 0 | W | H | E | R | E | | | | | | | | | | | | | | | | | | | | | |

The First Americans

Have you ever wondered **(0)** .... the first Americans came from? Until recently, archaeologists believed they had the answer to that question. Let's start with **(9)** .... we all know.

Many thousands of years **(10)** .... during the last Ice Age, sea levels dropped and revealed a land bridge linking Asia to Alaska. The result was that Asian tribes hunting horses and reindeer **(11)** .... now follow their prey into America.

(12) .... at the end of this period the ice melted and the sea covered the land bridge. The Asian hunters **(13)** .... now trapped in America. Over centuries, their descendants migrated north and south, and settled down in their new land.

But were **(14)** .... really the first Americans? Cave paintings **(15)** .... recently been found in Brazil. These depict animals which had **(16)** .... extinct long before the Asian tribes arrived – but they were clearly painted by someone!

So, were the Asian tribes really the first to settle in America? The answer may be less clear-cut than the archaeologists thought!

For questions **17–24**, read the text below. Use the word given in capitals at the end of some of the lines to form a word that fits in the gap **in the same line**. There is an example at the beginning (**0**).

In the exam, you write your answers **IN CAPITAL LETTERS on a separate answer sheet**.

Example: | 0 | A | R | G | U | M | E | N | T | S | | | | | | | | | | | | | | | |

Parents!

Do you have a lot of **(0)** .... with your parents? If you do, you're not alone. Mine drive me crazy! **ARGUE**

They often impose totally **(17)** .... rules, like making me come home as early as 8 p.m. every night, and then wonder **REASON**
why I **(18)** .... them and come home late. Honestly! I feel **OBEY**
like a **(19)** .... in my own home. **PRISON**

They have no respect for my **(20)** .... either. They're **PRIVATE**
always coming into my room without knocking, which is really
annoying. The way my dad behaves would make an angel feel
(21) .... , and I'm definitely no angel! **REBEL**

I've tried shouting and screaming, but **(22)** .... that make no **FORTUNATE**
difference at all. The only compromise is that Mum says when
I leave home I can make all my own **(23)** .... , but until then **DECIDE**
I have to do what I'm told. It's hard because I want my freedom
and **(24)** .... right now – I don't want to wait! **INDEPENDENT**

What on earth can I do?

Part 4

For questions **25–30**, complete the second sentence so that it has a similar meaning to the first sentence, using the word given. **Do not change the word given.** You must use between **two** and **five** words, including the word given. Here is an example (**0**).

Example:

0 My brother had a really good idea for our next holiday.
   CAME
   My brother .... really good idea for our next holiday.

The gap can be filled with the words 'came up with a', so you write:

Example: | **0** | CAME UP WITH A

In the exam, you write only the missing words **IN CAPITAL LETTERS on a separate answer sheet**.

_____

25 'I don't think you should miss school, Anna,' said Peter.
   ADVISED
   Peter .... school.

26 I last saw Julia a year ago.
   SINCE
   It's .... last saw Julia.

27 I'll only go if you do.
   UNLESS
   I .... do.

28 There's no time left.
   RUN
   We .... time.

29 It's not a good idea to do that, in my opinion.
   IF
   I wouldn't .... you.

30 I imagine it was difficult to give up eating chocolate.
   EASY
   It .... to give up eating chocolate.

You are going to read an extract from a story about a young sailor. For questions **31–36**, choose the answer (**A**, **B**, **C** or **D**) which you think fits best according to the text.

In the exam, you mark your answers **on a separate answer sheet**.

Castaway!

'Here we go again!' Alex yelled as yet another huge wave crashed onto his tiny boat, sending him sliding along the floor. If it weren't for the safety rope he was wearing, he'd have been flung into the ocean. Even now, it was far from certain that the boat would stay upright. The lightening flashed again, followed by the roar of the thunder. The storm was overhead now, gale-force winds whipping the angry waves into towering monsters.

Alex had known the voyage would be tough. Becoming the youngest sailor ever to cross the Pacific solo was no easy challenge. But he'd always been a brilliant sailor – everyone at the sailing club acknowledged that. And while they hadn't exactly encouraged him to take on this challenge, nobody had suggested he wasn't up to it except his headmaster, who had strongly objected to boys of his age making any such attempt. Luckily, his dad's promotion involved moving the family to a new country, so he'd managed to avoid the reach of the authorities, temporarily at least.

He'd thought nothing could make him feel fear when he was on the water. He'd faced all kinds of hazards over the years – sea fog, navigation problems, equipment failure – none had got the better of him. But this storm was something else! Never before had he felt so vulnerable in the face of nature. If he could only talk to somebody, this feeling of helplessness might decrease, but his communication system didn't seem to be working. 'Pull yourself together,' Alex told himself severely. 'The storm will be over soon.'

He was wrong. Instead of dying down, the winds grew stronger and waves the size of mountains spun the boat in every direction. Then, as Alex watched in horror, one truly gigantic wave rose up out of the ocean, crashed into the side of the boat and turned it right over. Struggling desperately to keep his head above water,

Alex pulled on the safety rope. Why was it so light? The reason quickly became clear. Instead of the whole boat, he was attached to just one small section of it. The boat had started to break up!

With an almost superhuman effort, Alex managed to drag his exhausted body onto the section of the boat he was tied to. There he lay as the storm raged round him until eventually stars began to appear in the sky and the winds died down. He must have drifted off to sleep – a troubled sleep from which he wakened every few minutes only to find his nightmare continuing. The sun was now high in the sky and his body began to burn with its heat. He was very thirsty, but apart from raindrops there was nothing to drink except sea water. But he knew what happened to shipwrecked sailors who did that – how the salt damaged their brains until they went crazy and died. It was a fate he did not aim to share.

Alex was drifting back into sleep when he became aware of a different sound – that of waves breaking. Opening his eyes, he saw something that made his heart beat fast. It was an island and was just a short swim away. He was safe! Using his hands as paddles, he steered himself to the shore where he threw himself upon the warm sand. For a while he relaxed in the joy of survival, but then reality hit him again. Was the island deserted and, if so, how was he going to survive? He'd heard of castaways who'd been trapped on islands like these for years with nobody knowing where they were. Was he going to suffer the same fate? With his heart in his mouth, he set off to explore his new home.

line 33

31 From the first paragraph, we understand that Alex

- **A** was enjoying the storm.
- **B** felt nervous about his boat.
- **C** was sure he was going to drown.
- **D** felt annoyed about his lack of preparation.

32 Who almost prevented Alex from making the trip?

- **A** The authorities.
- **B** The sailing club.
- **C** His father.
- **D** His headmaster.

33 The word 'vulnerable' in line 33 means

- **A** fearless.
- **B** determined.
- **C** defenceless.
- **D** impressed.

34 When the boat overturned, Alex discovered that

- **A** the safety rope had broken off.
- **B** he had not attached the rope correctly.
- **C** the rope was still tied to part of the boat.
- **D** the rope had disappeared in the sea.

35 In paragraph 5, we understand the biggest mistake Alex felt he could make would be to

- **A** drink sea water.
- **B** get too sunburnt.
- **C** catch raindrops.
- **D** fall asleep.

36 How did Alex feel after he arrived on the island?

- **A** Convinced that he was out of danger.
- **B** Surprised about making it to land.
- **C** Concerned about what would happen next.
- **D** Relieved that his ordeal was over.

You are going to read a magazine article about advertising. Six sentences have been removed from the article. Choose from the sentences **A–G** the one which fits each gap (**37–42**). There is one extra sentence which you do not need to use.

In the exam, you mark your answers **on a separate answer sheet**.

Advertising and you

We live in a materialistic world. Everywhere we look it seems there are images of celebrities wearing designer labels, or magazines and websites crammed with pictures of electronic devices that advertisers would like us to view as 'must have items'.

If you are a teenager, be very wary of advertising. These days, too many companies target their marketing strategies at young people. **37** Unless you get wise, learn to see through the marketing messages and become more critical of the tricks advertisers use, you will be an easy target. So, think before you spend your money! You wouldn't allow a stranger in the street to tell you what to buy – so why let the marketing industry get away with it?

38 That's unlikely. In our materialistic world, we are bombarded with adverts for twenty-four hours a day. You may be unaware of their effect, but that's because marketing strategies have become so clever. The marketers are at work, delving into our lives in ways you may never have realised. Have you ever done a quiz or answered a survey on the Internet? If you have, you may not be aware that your answers can be used by marketers to gather information about your spending habits and the products you are most likely to buy.

Advertisers have ensured that the desire for labeled, or branded, goods is common among teenagers. Clothes, accessories, electronic devices, … the list is endless. **39** Well, watch a professional football or tennis match and you'll see players wearing branded sports gear – what's the reason? It's not because they love the colour, style or fit. It's because the manufacturer is paying them huge sums of money to wear it.

This form of advertising, 'product placement', is an advertising strategy which aims to keep the consumer unaware that marketing is taking place. We probably don't notice that the hero of our favourite Hollywood blockbuster always wears jeans on which the maker's name is clearly displayed. **40** Then, when we next go out to buy new jeans, it will spring into the front of our minds and guide our choice.

Of course, most teenagers know deep down that wearing a 'label' does not make you a better, wiser, or more confident person – but peer pressure can be hard to resist. Teenagers, typically, feel insecure about their identity and image, so looking 'cool', powerful or 'one of the gang' becomes an issue of great importance. **41** Some teenagers think rebelling against authority will make them look even more 'cool'; marketers sometimes pick up on this and target them with ads for cigarettes or alcohol. But it's all a trick – they just end up smelling bad and ruining their health.

The biggest problem with advertising is that it can get inside your brain and persuade you to act in ways you really know are foolish. **42** Strong people are independent-minded: they realise that discovering a sense of identity – discovering who you are as a person and how you fit into society – is not something to be dictated by marketers. As individuals, we are worth much more than the advertisers would have us believe!

A But how do they persuade us we must buy particular brands?

B The ways that many companies market their products are pretty endless, too.

C Basing your identity on the brand you 'belong to' is actually a sign of weakness not strength.

D Their message is that you are what you own – and that buying 'stuff' will make you happier.

E However, the image of that particular brand will, the advertisers hope, rest in our subconscious.

F Advertisers know this and are quick to exploit the fact.

G Some people claim they pay no attention to advertising and never succumb to its aims.

Part 7

You are going to read an article about four teenage adventurers. For questions **43–52**, choose from the four teenagers (**A–D**). The teenagers may be chosen more than once.

In the exam, you mark your answers **on a separate answer sheet.**

Which teenage adventurer

had to continue to study during an expedition?	43
hopes to draw attention to an environmental issue?	44
wants to set an example for others?	45
feels proud of the recognition he received?	46
found physical problems less important than psychological ones?	47
wants to pass on a passion to others?	48
got the idea for an adventure from a picture?	49
needed to interrupt a journey due to mechanical problems?	50
was impressed by some animals he saw?	51
felt frustrated by being delayed by bad weather?	52

Teenage Adventurers

A Jordan Romero

Jordan was just thirteen when he became the youngest person to climb Mount Everest. This achievement formed another step in his bid to beat the world record and become the youngest person to climb the highest and most dangerous mountain peaks in the seven continents of the world. His inspiration came from a painting in his school hall. Jordan feels proud of what he has achieved and wants it to stand as a model to show that anything is possible. But his activities have renewed controversy over how much freedom young record-breakers should be given to undertake adventures that are becoming ever more ambitious. While Jordan trained for years to achieve his latest feat, many young teens dream of breaking similar records with only minimal preparation and little experience of the trials they will meet.

B Parker Liautaud

Nineteen-year-old Parker was still at college when he became the youngest – and the fastest – man to ski to the North Pole. Despite being held up at the start by poor climatic conditions, which was hard to deal with, he later managed the feat in just eighteen days. Parker suffered from backache and skin problems on the expedition, but he said his biggest challenge was a mental one: learning how to handle uncertainty and danger. He is one of a seemingly ever-growing bunch of teenage adventurers who are determined to test themselves to the extreme in order to break a world record. It's not just personal glory that drove Parker, though. He wants to raise awareness of the problems of global warming. His regular live updates on this journey certainly helped in this effort.

C Mike Perham

By the time seventeen-year-old Mike Perham crossed the finishing line that marked the end of his solo voyage round the world, he had spent 158 days at sea. In doing so, he broke the record for the youngest sailor to circumnavigate the world alone. His adventure was not without problems: he had to make stops in foreign ports due to equipment failure, battle stormy seas, and struggle with acute loneliness, while not neglecting the coursework his college set him to complete when he was away. On the positive side, he had amazing and inspirational encounters with marine creatures, including a large group of friendly dolphins that came and swam beside his boat. In setting his record, Mike showed he had both mental and physical stamina without which he could never have achieved his dream.

D Ryan Campbell

When teenage pilot Ryan set out to become the youngest person to fly solo round the globe in a single engine aircraft on 'The Teen World Flight', he could never have imagined the challenges that would face him. Flying over fifteen countries meant obtaining landing permits and struggling to obtain aviation fuel during his frequent stops. On one occasion, he had to deal with the dangerous situation of ice on his wings. For his achievement, the teenager was given an award, of which he is justifiably proud. Ryan, whose three brothers also fly, is keen to support other teenagers who also want to be pilots – or pursue any other dreams of adventure!

Part 1

You **must** answer this question. Write your answer in **140–190** words in an appropriate style.

In the exam, you write your answer **on a separate answer sheet**.

1   In your English class, you have been talking about the advantages and disadvantages of using social networking sites. Now your teacher has asked you to write an essay.

Write your essay using **all** the notes and give reasons for your point of view.

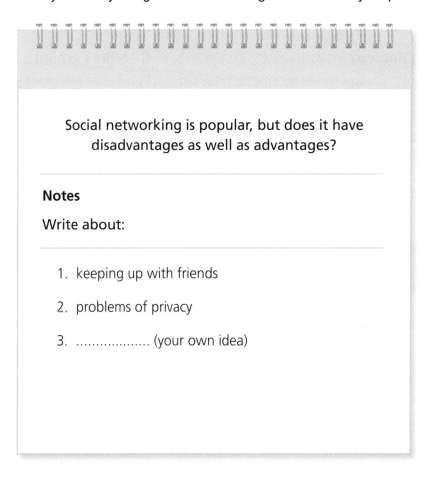

Social networking is popular, but does it have disadvantages as well as advantages?

Notes

Write about:

1. keeping up with friends

2. problems of privacy

3. .... (your own idea)

Part 2

Write an answer to **one** of the questions 2–5 in this part. Write your answer in **140–190** words in an appropriate style.

In the exam, you write your answer **on a separate answer sheet**. Put the question number in the box at the top of the answer sheet.

2 You have seen this announcement on an English language website for schools.

> ## Articles Wanted!
> ### *How important is technology to today's teenagers?*
> Write an article for the website about the kind of devices that
> are popular with teenagers in your school or town,
> explaining which you think are most useful,
> and mentioning some of the downsides to using them.

Write your **article**.

3 You have seen this announcement on a website for teenagers.

> **Story Competition**
> Enter our short story competition! The best story will win a laptop!
> Your story must begin with this sentence:
> **Ann felt her heart miss a beat when she realised
> the boat was letting in water.**
> Your story must include: • a surprise • a rescue

Write your **story**.

4 This is part of a letter you have received from your English friend, Elena.

> *Can you help me? I'm doing a school project on the things young
> people like to do when they're away on holiday. Can you tell me about
> the things you do on holiday and why you like doing them?*
> *Thanks, Elena*

Write your **letter**.

5 Answer the following question based on the title below.

> ***The Eagle of the Ninth* by Rosemary Sutcliff**
> In your English class, you have been discussing the story of
> *The Eagle of the Ninth*. Now your teacher has asked you to write
> a review for the school magazine.
> Describe some of the plot of the book *The Eagle of the Ninth*
> and say whether you would recommend it to your fellow
> students and why.

Write your **review**.

Part 1

You will hear people talking in eight different situations. For questions **1–8**, choose the best answer (**A**, **B** or **C**).

1   You hear a drama teacher talking about teaching Shakespeare's plays.
    What does she say about them?

    A   They take a lot of time to understand completely.
    B   They make more sense when they are acted not read.
    C   They are often taught in schools to students who are too young.

2   You hear two people talking about an entertainment centre.
    What does the man think the centre should do?

    A   Increase the number of activities on offer.
    B   Extend the opening hours.
    C   Publicise the booking system more.

3   You hear a message on a telephone answering machine.
    Why is the speaker calling?

    A   To get an opinion.
    B   To cancel an arrangement.
    C   To confirm an existing plan.

4   You hear a teenager talking about climbing Everest.
    How does he feel about the danger?

    A   Upset when others are concerned about it.
    B   Worried about it when climbing very high.
    C   Intent on facing it and doing well.

5   You hear two teenagers talking about a film they have seen.
    What do they both think about the film?

    A   Some parts were frightening.
    B   The plot was difficult to follow.
    C   A few characters were unbelievable.

6   You hear two people talking in a shop.
    Why is the man there?

    A   To get some advice.
    B   To apologise about something.
    C   To make a complaint.

7   You hear two people taking about a TV programme.
    What do they agree about the programme?

    A   There was not enough about the environment.
    B   The photography was exceptional.
    C   The harsh reality of life in the Arctic was clearly shown.

8   You hear part of a radio programme.
    What is the presenter doing?

    A   Alerting listeners to traffic problems.
    B   Delivering a detailed weather forecast.
    C   Describing floods in some parts of the country.

Part 2

You will hear a boy called Peter giving a class presentation on the subject of his ideal job. For questions **9–18**, complete the sentences with a word or short phrase.

My ideal job

Peter was surprised that it was the **(9)** ....

where he found the best information.

Peter uses the word **(10)** .... to describe how

he thinks of the theatre.

It was Peter's **(11)** .... who really started

his interest in live theatre.

Peter describes the feeling of being on stage as

(12) ....

Peter felt embarrassed when he forgot to give an actor a

(13) .... to take on stage.

Peter has learned the importance of **(14)** ....

for a stage manager.

According to Peter, it's sorting out **(15)** ....

that he really enjoys.

Peter discovered that producers often like stage managers with lots of

(16) ....

Peter has heard that **(17)** .... can sometimes

be difficult to work with.

According to Peter, being **(18)** .... is the most

important quality for a stage manager.

Part 3

You will hear five short extracts in which young adventurers are talking about their experiences. For questions **19–23**, choose from the list (**A–H**) how each speaker feels about the experience. Use the letters only once. There are three extra letters which you do not need to use.

A It's important to expose young people to some risks.

Speaker 1 | 19 |

B I saw the adventure as a way of improving my fitness.

Speaker 2 | 20 |

C I was driven on by the support I was given.

Speaker 3 | 21 |

D I don't think experience matters if you're determined to succeed.

Speaker 4 | 22 |

E I'm not bothered about performing better than anyone else.

Speaker 5 | 23 |

F I wasn't very keen on my first taste of adventure.

G It was my teacher that inspired me to go on the adventure.

H It took a lot of physical preparation.

Part 4

You will hear a radio interview with a man called John Wilson, who is talking about his work as a fire fighter. For questions **24–30**, choose the best answer (**A**, **B** or **C**).

24 What does John say about his everyday work?

   A He is surprised by some of the work he has to do.
   B He feels nervous dealing with certain situations.
   C He gets angry when people misunderstand what his job involves.

25 How does John feel about the amount of technology in his job?

   A He thinks it will never totally replace the need for paperwork.
   B He feels unsure about how useful it is away from the fire station.
   C He's convinced it saves time in the long run.

26 John says that updating technical information

   A is not done during busy times at the fire station.
   B is not easy to do on a regular basis.
   C is not something he has to do.

27 According to John, the procedure for dealing with emergency calls

   A is faster than it was in the past.
   B often helps to deal with a hoax calls.
   C works best when a specialist operator takes the call.

28 What does John say about the fire engines he uses?

   A They are adapted to deal with different types of emergency.
   B They are often difficult to handle in busy cities.
   C They can only be driven by certain people.

29 Why does John tell the story of the cat up the tree?

   A It was the most unusual thing that had happened to him.
   B It made a serious point about using the fire service.
   C It showed why he feels his job is important.

30 What does John appreciate most about technology?

   A The speed with which it works.
   B The reduction of danger it brings.
   C The financial benefits it creates.

PART 1 (2 minutes)

Good morning/afternoon/evening. My name is … and this is my colleague … .

And your names are?

- Where are you from, *(Candidate A)*?
- And you, *(Candidate B)*?

First, we'd like to know something about you.

Select one or more questions from any of the following categories, as appropriate.

Sport

- **What's your favourite sport? (Why?)**
- **Do you enjoy the same kinds of sport as your friends? (Why/Why not?)**
- **How often do you watch sport on television? (Why?)**
- **Do you do sport after school? (Why/Why not?)**

Personal preferences

- **Do you like your school? (Why/Why not?)**
- **What's your favourite subject at school? (Why?)**
- **What kinds of things do you enjoy reading? (Why?)**
- **Tell us about your best friend.**

Celebrations

- **What did you do on your last birthday? (Why?)**
- **Tell us about a local festival in your town.**
- **Have you been to any good parties recently? (Why/Why not?)**
- **Tell us about a family celebration you really enjoyed.**

In this part of the test, I'm going to give each of you two photographs. I'd like you to talk about your photographs on your own for about a minute, and also to answer a question about your partner's photographs.

(Candidate A), it's your turn first. Here are your photographs. They show **people doing fun things in different places**. [*Turn to the pictures on page 52.*]. I'd like you to compare the photographs, and say **why you think the people have chosen to have fun in these places.** All right?

(1 minute)

Thank you. *(Candidate B),* **which of these places would you prefer to have fun in? (Why?)**

(30 seconds)

Thank you. Now, *(Candidate B),* here are your photographs. They show **people learning about the past in different ways**. [*Turn to the pictures on page 53.*] I'd like you to compare the photographs, and say **why you think the people have decided to learn about the past in these ways.** All right?

(1 minute)

Thank you. *(Candidate A),* **in which of these ways would you prefer to learn about the past? (Why?)**

(30 seconds)

Thank you.

Now I'd like you to talk about something together for about two minutes.

Here are some ways advertisers choose to advertise their products for teenagers, and a question for you to discuss. First, you have some time to look at the task. [*Turn to the task on page 54.*]

(15 seconds)

Now, talk to each other about whether these ways of advertising products for teenagers are really effective.

(2 minutes)

Thank you. Now you have a minute to decide **which way of advertising is most effective for teenagers.**

(1 minute)

Use the following questions in order, as appropriate:

- **Do you think there are too many advertisements everywhere? (Why/Why not?)**

- **Do you usually buy something because you've seen it advertised, or because your friends have it? (Why?)**

- **Do you think schools should teach students about the way advertising works? (Why/Why not?)**

- **Is there an advertisement you've seen recently that you really liked? (Why/Why not?)**

- **Why do you think young people enjoy spending free time in shopping malls?**

- **Some people say we all buy too many things. Do you agree? (Why/Why not?)**

Thank you. That is the end of the test.

> *Select any of the following prompts, as appropriate:*
>
> - **What do you think?**
> - **Do you agree?**
> - **And you?**

Visuals for Speaking Tests

Test 1: Part 2, Student A

Why have the people chosen to do these sporting activities with friends?

What are the people enjoying about having a holiday in these places?

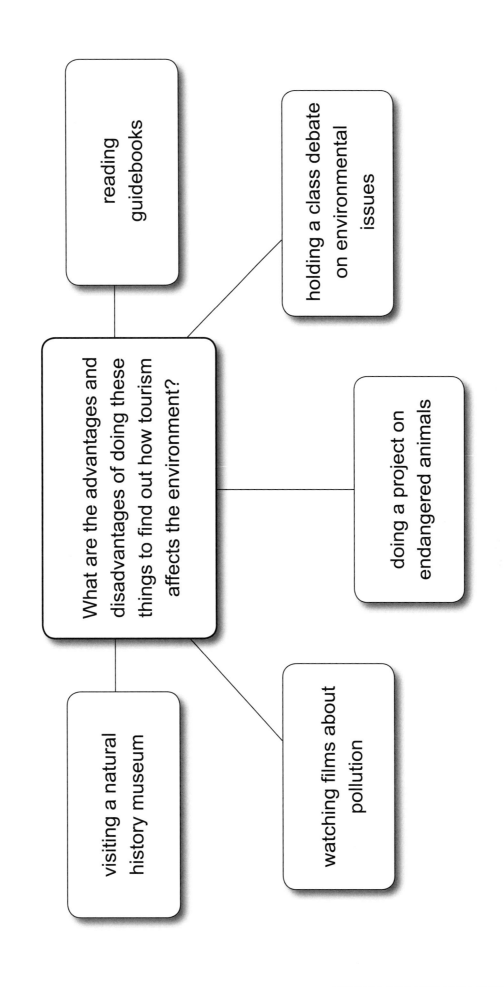

reading guidebooks

holding a class debate on environmental issues

What are the advantages and disadvantages of doing these things to find out how tourism affects the environment?

doing a project on endangered animals

visiting a natural history museum

watching films about pollution

Why have the people chosen to have fun in these places?

Why have the people decided to learn about the past in these ways?

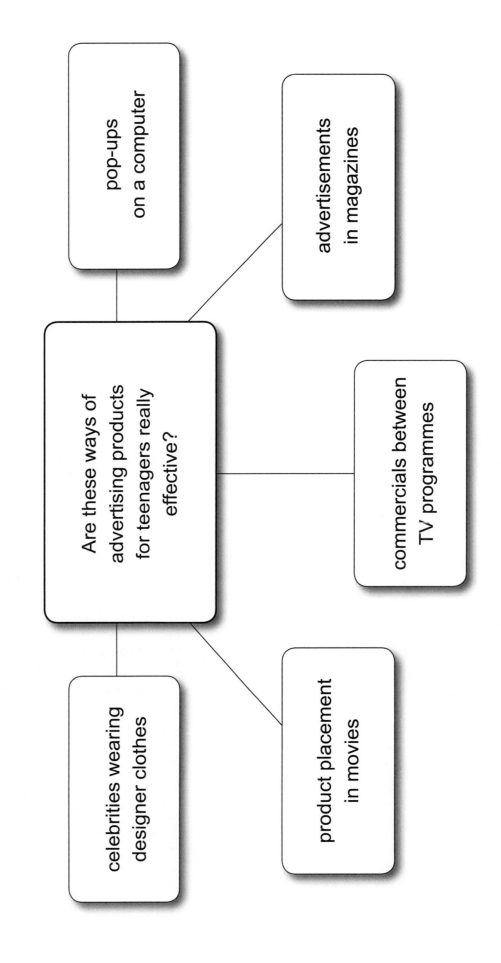

pop-ups
on a computer

advertisements
in magazines

Are these ways of
advertising products
for teenagers really
effective?

commercials between
TV programmes

celebrities wearing
designer clothes

product placement
in movies

Speaking and Writing Banks

Part 1

In this part of the test, you answer a few questions on personal topics such as your home, your daily routine, your work, likes and dislikes, etc.

Useful language

Communicative strategies

Sorry, can you say that again?

Sorry, I didn't quite catch that.

Could you repeat that, please?

Do you mean ... ?

Well, that depends on …

That's an interesting question.

No, I'm afraid I don't like that much.

Absolutely!

Now, how can I put this?

Giving personal information

I like to keep in touch with friends. That's why my phone is so important to me.

I've always (dis)liked … . I'm not sure why.

To be honest, I'm not very good at …

Actually, I don't really enjoy …

My house is rather small but very comfortable.

I'm an only child and I live with my parents.

Responding to questions about everyday life and interests

Although I love sport, I don't do much regularly because …

I have to do some housework; all the family have to help out.

I've never played a musical instrument, but I'd love to learn the … because …

I haven't made a final decision yet, but I'd really like to ... in the future.

I'm not very sure what I'll do, but I may decide to …

My parents want me to …

I used to be very keen on ... , but now I prefer …

I don't like … , though I do enjoy …

Exam help

- Give your answers confidently, and add interesting details or examples. Remember not to say too much, though – your answers should not be too long in this part.

- Avoid making basic grammar mistakes. Think about the verb tense you are going to use: should you speak about the past, the present or the future?

- Speak clearly so that your partner and the two examiners can hear and understand everything you say.

- Don't try to add anything to what your partner says – these questions are for each of you to answer individually.

Part 2

In this part of the test, you speak on your own for one minute. You compare two photographs and answer an additional question about them.

Useful language

Comparing

The people in these photos are in very different places.

In the first photograph they're … , whereas in the second …

The people are doing completely different activities …

These are very different ways of …

I can see some similarities in these photos, for example, the people in both pictures are friends.

The people in the first photograph look happier than the others because ...

The man in the café seems to be having a better time than ...

There's a clear difference between these two photos; one of them is … , whilst the other …

I don't think the people in the first photograph are as relaxed as those in the second.

Speculating

I may be wrong, but I think they are probably close friends.

We don't know what they're looking at, but I suppose …

Perhaps they've decided to share this because …

The students seem to be enjoying each other's company.

I get the impression that the woman …

The girl looks as though she's feeling …

The boy may have decided to read here because …

I think the girl looks really tired, maybe she's been studying all day.

The students in the first photograph are probably …

I think the girl may be feeling stressed because …

Exam help

- Remember not to describe the photos, but to compare them. You don't have time to comment in detail on each photo individually. Start by comparing the people, the places and the situations, and remember that the examiner has told you what the pictures are about in their instructions.

- After you have compared the photographs, use the question written above the photographs to remind yourself about the second part of the task. In this part, you should say what you think, and give your opinion with reasons. Make sure you answer the question and don't just talk about your personal reaction to the pictures.

- Use varied vocabulary and grammatical structures, and try to use comparative forms correctly.

- If there's a word in the photographs you don't know or can't remember, don't worry – explain what you want to say in a different way.

Part 3

In this part of the test, you complete a task with your partner. You discuss the different written prompts in turn, and respond to each other's comments and ideas.

Useful language

Inviting your partner to give their opinion

Some of these ideas don't seem very practical. What do you think?

I don't know about you, but in my opinion …

I'd hate to do that. Do you agree with me?

You may disagree with me, but I think …

What do you think?

Is this a better idea, do you think?

Why do you think that's a good idea?

Can you explain why you think that?

Responding to your partner's opinions

I'm sure most students would like to do that.

Sorry, I think that would be a waste of time.

Well, in my opinion, … is more important.

That's an interesting point, but we also need to consider …

That's a good point, but don't you think it might be useful to … ?

As you said, … might be a good thing. However, …

I take your point, but I still think …

I'm afraid I don't agree. I really believe that …

Well, I'd say that …

Moving to another written prompt

Right, why don't we talk about … ?

How about this idea? Do you want to say something about it?

What do you think about this idea?

Now, moving on, we haven't talked about … yet.

Shall we discuss this idea next?

We've probably said enough about that, don't you think?

I'd like to say something about …

- Focus on the task you've been given, and discuss the options for about two minutes. You don't need to talk about all the prompts, so if you have a lot to say about one, don't rush to include them all. It's more important to have a good discussion than cover all the prompts.

- Look at the question printed in the central box which will help you stay focused on the task.

- Remember that, after the two-minute discussion, the examiner will give you a second question to discuss for a minute which will involve making a decision. Don't make the decision too quickly because, then, you may not find other things to say.

- When your partner gives his/her opinion on a written prompt, respond fully before moving to something else. You can agree, disagree or add more ideas to support what he/she has said.

- If your partner seems happy to let you do most of the talking, try to involve him/her by asking his/her opinions. You will be given credit for doing that.

Part 4

In this part of the test, you take part in a discussion by answering questions which broaden the topic of Part 3. You can respond to what your partner says when he/she is answering a question from the examiner.

Useful language

Giving opinions

Well, personally, I feel …

People often say that … , but I ...

Young people often complain that … and I agree.

I don't think teenagers should be prevented from doing things.

I'd suggest doing something different …

I think it's unlikely that anybody would …

Yes, I think young people have much more freedom than …

I think some people find it really difficult to …

No, that's not the way I see things.

I'm not sure, to be honest.

My friends think I'm wrong, but I believe …

Let's be optimistic about the future and say that …

Giving examples and/or reasons

I can think of a few examples of this …

Let me try to explain why …

For example, when you …

I once had an experience which …

To show you what I mean, I can give you …

There are many reasons for this …

People don't like this idea. I think that's because …

When you're young you can be adventurous. That's why I …

Just think of all the challenges young people face; to begin with …

Adding to what your partner has said

You said … , and I agree with that.

Yes, you're right, and what's more …

I can add something to that.

I'd like to say something more about that.

Can I give another example of what he's/she's said?

Exam help

- Remember these questions require more extended responses than those in Part 1.

- Don't be afraid to talk about your opinions and feelings. The examiner wants you to produce complex language that will show off what you can do.

- There's no 'correct' answer to the questions. You won't be assessed on what you think, only on how you say it. Try to always give reasons and examples to back up your opinions.

- You can contribute ideas to what your partner says, even if the examiner did not ask you the question.

Part 1: Essay

Exam question

In your English class, you have been talking about what it means to be famous and how fame can affect a person's life. Now your English teacher has asked you to write an essay.

Write your essay using **all** the notes and give reasons for your point of view. Write your answer in **140–190** words in an appropriate style.

How easy or difficult is life for people who suddenly become celebrities?

Notes

Write about:

1. a life of luxury

2. lack of privacy

3. .... (your own idea)

Useful language

Introduction

You often hear people say that …

There are arguments for and against this idea.

People often disagree about whether it is …

This is an important topic that needs to be discussed …

Speculative language

They may attract attention on social media.

They could be unfairly criticised …

They might be subjected to attacks.

Some unhappiness may be hidden …

Conclusion

To sum up, I will say that …

Taking all this into account, I believe …

Having discussed different points of view, it seems clear that …

Finally, I have come to the conclusion that …

Sample answer

Start your essay with a sentence introducing the topic of the essay.	**How easy or difficult is life for people who suddenly become celebrities?**

How easy or difficult is life for people who suddenly become celebrities?

▶ When somebody becomes a celebrity more or less overnight, their life will change. Some changes will be positive, some negative.

First of all, celebrity status usually means lots of money as celebrities get innumerable offers of work to appear on television and promote and advertise luxury goods. Having so much wealth may seem like a dream, but it could cause problems, such as false friends who are only interested in the celebrity's money. ◀

▶ Secondly, there is the unavoidable loss of privacy. Celebrities are recognised in the street, so they are not able to hide anywhere. People will ask them for autographs and want to take selfies with them. Whilst some people love that sort of attention, others may find it unbearable, particularly if it also affects their families. ◀

▶ Finally, celebrities may attract negative attention and comments on social media, where they could be unfairly criticised or subjected to attacks. They may even become the object of envy and hatred.

To sum up, it seems to me that celebrities lead a life of luxury and receive a lot of public attention, but we often don't see how much unhappiness may be hidden behind the happy exterior. ◀

Using linking words such as 'Secondly' or 'Finally' will help you organise your ideas clearly.

Make sure you add an idea of your own.

Use one paragraph for each topic.

Use varied language and some complex sentences, but keep a semi-formal style.

Your conclusion should be a summary of the opinions you have given earlier.

Exam help

- Read the question carefully and plan what you want to include in four or five clear paragraphs.

- Write down some interesting ideas for each paragraph, together with some language you may want to use. You should try to use varied vocabulary that is relevant to the topic, and to include some complex sentences using linking words.

- Remember that you're presenting your point of view and you need to support it with some reasons, examples or evidence.

- Use a formal or semi-formal style, and avoid using informal language.

Aim to write five paragraphs:

Paragraph 1

The introduction: Try to write two sentences to avoid a single-sentence paragraph. The first sentence can be a re-phrasing of the essay title. The second sentence can be a brief summary of what you are going to say.

Paragraph 2

Deal with the first note: a life of luxury.

Paragraph 3

Deal with the second note: lack of privacy.

Paragraph 4

Deal with the third note (your own): being criticised on social media.

Paragraph 5

The conclusion. Summarise your main points from paragraphs 2, 3 and 4. Try to write at least two sentences to avoid a single-sentence paragraph.

Each note will be just a few words long. The note on its own will not give you enough to write about. Before you start writing, take a few minutes to expand them. Here is one way to do it:

1   Write down the notes (including your own) and draw three lines from each one. Now concentrate on each note in turn. Try to think of three ideas that can add content to that note. For example:

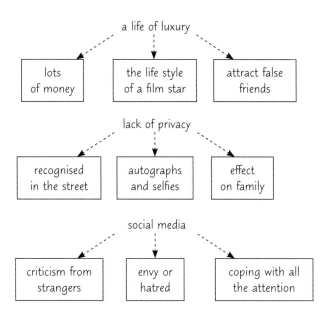

2   Choose the best ideas from your notes and start writing.

When you have finished writing your essay, use this checklist.

Content

Have you covered **both** the two notes given <u>and</u> added **one** of your own?

Communicative achievement

Is your style correct for an essay, i.e. is it fairly formal? Are your opinions easy to follow?

Organisation

Have you divided your writing into paragraphs, with an introduction and a conclusion?

Does your conclusion follow the arguments in your essay logically?

Language

Have you used:

•   some complex sentences with linking words?

•   a variety of grammatical structures and tenses?

•   some interesting vocabulary?

Part 2: Article

Exam question

You recently saw this announcement on a teenage website.

> ### Articles wanted!
> ### CAN YOU WRITE AN ARTICLE ON THIS TOPIC AND HELP MILLIONS OF STUDENTS?
>
> How to avoid stress when you're studying hard
> - ○ How do you organise your work?
> - ○ What do you do to relax?
> - ○ What other useful tip do you have to avoid stress?

Write your **article**.
Write your answer in **140–190** words in an appropriate style.

Sample answer

You can use direct or indirect questions to add interest.

This is a clear way to introduce the second point you have to include.

Take action to beat stress now!

Give your article a catchy or interesting title to attract attention and make people want to read it.

Do you find yourself getting more and more anxious while studying? Read on because this page may change your life!

The first thing is to organise your work. This is how I do it: I divide my work into manageable chunks, so that a task that seems enormous becomes a series of smaller tasks. Think of the question: 'How do you eat an elephant?' Well, what's the answer? It's 'bit by bit'. So simple and yet so clever!

Using questions like this engages the readers by talking to them directly.

The next step: relaxation. It's not enough to say, 'I'll relax for a few minutes.' You have to take relaxation seriously! Think of an activity that gives you real pleasure. In my case, this means taking some chocolate and finding the quietest place in the house or garden where I can sit or lie and listen to my favourite music for a while. Let it clear your head of all thoughts.

Finally, one more tip: share the burden of studying! Invite a friend you get on really well with – it must be somebody who is on the same wavelength as you. Discuss the difficult points of your work and give each other lots of support.

Good luck!

Finish your article in an interesting way that involves the reader.

Useful language

Rhetorical questions

Do you find yourself getting anxious … ?

How would you answer this question?

Are you ready for change? Then, …

How about doing something that will change your life?

Addressing the reader directly

Read on because this may change your life!

Share the burden of studying!

You have to take relaxation seriously!

Think of this question.

Good luck!

Giving examples from personal experience

This is how I do it.

In my case, this means taking/going …

Personally, I prefer to …

I can say this from experience …

Exam help

- Read the question carefully and plan your article before you start to write. Pay attention to who you are writing your article for. If it's for your school magazine, you can use an informal style. If it's for a magazine with a wider readership, you may need a semi-formal style.

- Write down some interesting language you could use. Remember that the purpose of your article is not only to inform, but also to entertain the reader.

- Think of an interesting title.

- Use interesting details, examples or brief stories/anecdotes to give your article a personal touch.

Part 2: Email

Exam question

You have received an email from your English-speaking friend, Sam, who is doing a presentation at school about teenagers' lives in different parts of the world. Write an email to Sam, answering his questions.

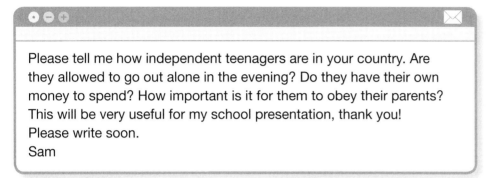

Please tell me how independent teenagers are in your country. Are they allowed to go out alone in the evening? Do they have their own money to spend? How important is it for them to obey their parents? This will be very useful for my school presentation, thank you!
Please write soon.
Sam

Write your **email**.
Write your answer in **140–190** words in an appropriate style.

Sample answer

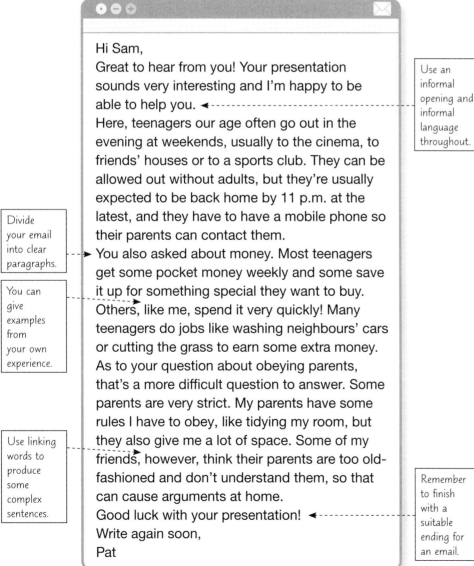

Hi Sam,
Great to hear from you! Your presentation sounds very interesting and I'm happy to be able to help you. ◄

Use an informal opening and informal language throughout.

Here, teenagers our age often go out in the evening at weekends, usually to the cinema, to friends' houses or to a sports club. They can be allowed out without adults, but they're usually expected to be back home by 11 p.m. at the latest, and they have to have a mobile phone so their parents can contact them.

Divide your email into clear paragraphs.

You also asked about money. Most teenagers get some pocket money weekly and some save it up for something special they want to buy.

You can give examples from your own experience.

Others, like me, spend it very quickly! Many teenagers do jobs like washing neighbours' cars or cutting the grass to earn some extra money. As to your question about obeying parents, that's a more difficult question to answer. Some parents are very strict. My parents have some rules I have to obey, like tidying my room, but they also give me a lot of space. Some of my friends, however, think their parents are too old-fashioned and don't understand them, so that can cause arguments at home.

Use linking words to produce some complex sentences.

Good luck with your presentation! ◄

Remember to finish with a suitable ending for an email.

Write again soon,
Pat

Useful language

Informal openings
Dear Sam,
Hello Sam,
Hi Sam,

Introducing a new point
You also asked about …
Now, to answer your question about …
As to your question about money, …
Moving on to your question about …
Finally, you wanted to know …

Agreeing to help
I'm happy to be able to help …
I'll do my best to help you …
I'm not an expert, but …
I can help you by looking up more …
Whatever I can do …

Wishing good luck
Good luck with your presentation!
I hope your presentation goes really well!
Let me know how your presentation goes!
I'm sure your presentation will be a success!

Exam help

- Read the instructions and the email very carefully, noting down all the information you need to include in your answer.

- Decide what to include in each paragraph. Jot down some vocabulary you may want to use.

- Try to write close to the maximum number of words by adding details.

- Remember you are writing an email to a friend, so your relationship with your reader is personal and informal.

Part 2: Review

Exam question

You see a notice in a magazine for students of English.

Write a review for us
and you could see it published in our next issue!

Do you watch programmes for a teenage audience
on TV or the Internet? Is there one that you particularly like?
Tell us about the programme, what makes it special for you,
and whether you would recommend it to teenagers and young adults.

Write your **review**.
Write your answer in **140–190** words in an appropriate style.

Sample answer

If you want a show that's both interesting and funny, look no further. 'Simple Things' is about Robin, a teenager, and his friends. Robin isn't an ordinary teenager, he's someone with a wicked sense of humour who can play the drums. The plot is about his attempts to become a pop star whilst helping his friends solve their problems.

What makes it so special for me? I love the humour in it. Whatever the problems, the different characters always have a positive, upbeat message. And Robin's jokes are so funny they never fail to make me laugh. You feel that you are there with them, laughing in the same room.

There's something else. There is humour, but there's also drama and tension between the characters. It's often helped me understand my own problems better because some of the characters are such good role models. I often ask myself, 'What would I do in that situation? Would I do what Robin does?'

If you're over twenty, forget it. But I'd recommend it without hesitation to anybody between thirteen and nineteen. But, I must warn you, it's so good it can become addictive!

Use your imagination! You can invent things like the name or content of the programme.

Always give examples to back up your opinions.

Don't be afraid to express your personal views.

You can address the reader directly as you are expressing opinions in a persuasive way.

Don't forget you'll need a couple of lines for the last part of the task – in a review it may well be whether you recommend it or not.

Useful language

Introducing the plot
This is about …
This tells the story of a boy …
We learn about the relationships …
This programme takes the viewer to …
The programme is set in … (time/place)

Expressing enthusiasm
I love the humour in this …
It never fails to amuse me …
You won't believe how good this is …
It's so good it can become addictive …
It's incredibly memorable …

Recommending
I recommend this without hesitation …
If you want to … , look no further.
I wouldn't recommend this to anyone over the age of …
If you like comedies, this show is definitely for you.

Exam help

- Read the question carefully and plan your review before you start to write. Think of the style you will use, which will probably be semi-formal.

- Use varied language, including interesting adjectives. Note down some words you may want to use to avoid using words like 'good' or 'nice' all the time. You need to use varied language, including interesting adjectives, to engage the reader.

- Think about how you can organise the content into paragraphs. You need to include several things within the question: inform the reader about the programme, give your personal opinion and say whether you would recommend it.

- Check your spelling and punctuation, and correct any basic errors you may have made.

Part 2: Story

Exam question

You have seen this announcement in your school's student magazine.

Stories wanted

We want short stories for the school magazine!
Your story must begin with this sentence:

*As soon as she realised what the date was,
Carrie began to panic.*

Your story must include:
- a complaint
- a present

Write your **story**.
Write your answer in **140–190** words in an appropriate style.

Sample answer

> Make sure that your first sentence continues from the given sentence clearly and logically.

As soon as she realised what the date was, Carrie began to panic. It couldn't be the week before her father's birthday already! She knew that this was a special year, but she had been relying on her older sister to remind her to send a card, and to organise a party.

> Try to use a range of verbs, adverbs and adjectives to make your story interesting.

She rushed to her bag, grabbed her mobile phone, and frantically dialled her sister. The moment she answered, Carrie began to complain angrily. 'Why didn't you call me? I nearly forgot!' Her sister told her calmly that everything was in hand – the party was going to be held the following Saturday at a restaurant, but it was a secret and their father mustn't know. Carrie felt so relieved!

> Use a variety of structures such as reported/direct speech, and idioms.

> Use sequencing words to make sure the narrative is clear.

Now, all she had to do was buy a present for her father. She wandered round the local shops, but could see nothing he might like. Then, suddenly, she had an idea. Ringing her sister again, they agreed to buy him the famous book of wildlife photographs Carrie knew he'd always wanted.

> Include a final sentence or two that brings the story to a conclusion.

So, a day that had nearly been a disaster turned out well in the end!

Useful language

Use interesting vocabulary

She rushed to her bag, grabbed the mobile phone and frantically dialled her sister.

Her sister told her calmly …

She wandered round the shops …

Sequence the story clearly

As soon as …

The moment she …

Now, ….

Then, suddenly, …

No sooner had she … than …

After that, …

Finishing the story

So, …

Finally she realised …

It all became clear, and she realised …

In the end, it had all been a mistake …

Exam help

- Read the question carefully and plan the whole story before you start to write. Think about how you want to end your story, so that the narrative is logical and easy to follow.

- Make sure your story follows the given sentence logically and clearly, and the reader can easily see the connection between them.

- Remember you have to show a range of language, so use interesting vocabulary such as adverbs, adjectives and verbs. Vary the construction of your sentences to add interest, and remember you can include idioms if they are appropriate for the style of your story.

- Include a conclusion that rounds off your story nicely – don't just stop when you've written 190 words. Make the ending a vital part of your narrative!

Part 2: Set text – article

Exam question

> ***The Eagle of The Ninth*** by Rosemary Sutcliffe
>
> In your English class you have been discussing the story of 'The Eagle of the Ninth'. Now your teacher has asked you to write an article for the school magazine.
>
> Describe some parts of the story you thought were important. Why did you enjoy it so much?

Write your **article**.
Write your answer in **140–190** words in an appropriate style.

Sample answer

In the first paragraph, involve your reader by using a rhetorical question.

A novel to enjoy

Do you enjoy historical novels and stories with lots of action? Try this one!

'The Eagle of the Ninth' by Rosemary Sutcliff is set in Roman Britain, and centres around a young garrison commander called Marcus Aquila. He is clearly very brave because in one scene in the early part of the story he attacked an enemy chariot on his own. The Ninth Legion had been mysteriously lost many years earlier, and at that time Marcus' father had been part of it. The most important storyline involves Marcus' attempts to uncover the answer to what happened to his father and also to find the missing Roman Eagle standard – this is important and is also the title of the novel. Marcus spends a lot of the story in disguise, which is an important aspect of his adventures.

Give examples from the book to support your ideas.

Explain why some things you choose to write about are important.

I particularly enjoyed the story, because it combines action, mystery and adventure. It is also a romantic novel, because we follow the developing romance between Marcus and Cottia, but this is an added interest to the exciting plot.

Give your overall opinion of the book.

All in all, it is a really gripping book, and one to read again and again.

Include a final sentence or two summarising your views of the book.

Useful language

Giving examples from the book

He is clearly brave because in one scene he …

The most important storyline involves …

Marcus spends a lot of the story in disguise because …

It is a romantic novel because …

The most exciting scene is …

I remember the scene where … very clearly because …

The best example of mystery is the part where …

A good example of this is when Marcus …

The scene when Marcus … shows that he …

Using interesting language

I particularly enjoyed …

… which had been mysteriously lost.

… uncover the answer …

… it combines action, mystery and adventure.

Exam help

- Remember that the question on the set text can be an article, a review, a letter or an essay. Read the question carefully to identify what type of question it is, and plan your answer before you start to write.

- The question may ask you to write about things like the characters, scenes, or the storyline. Decide how many paragraphs you will need and what information from the set text you will include in each.

- Remember you have to show a range of language, so use interesting vocabulary and write full sentences, linking your ideas to produce some complex sentences. Support all your ideas with examples from the set text.

- Write a conclusion, even if it is short.